BIBLE VR

UNDERSTANDING VR FOR FAITH BASED EDUCATION AND ENTERTAINMENT

Dr. Pearry Teo, Ph.D, Min.D, Ed.D, CSC

DEDICATION

The amazing people who brought Bible VR into reality and to everybody who believes in VR as a way of the future for faith based learning.

Specifically, I want to thank my father, Tony Teo, for believing in me, without him, none of this would be a reality. He has been my dad, mentor and spiritual advisor.

CONTENTS

INTRODUCTION

I will not set before my eyes anything that is worthless. I hate the work of those who fall away; it shall not cling to me."

Psalms 101:3

In today's world filled with hectic lives and busy schedules, parents have relied more heavily on media as a tool to help them in their parenting. You'll see it all around you as you stroll into a restaurant and see a young kid staring quietly into his or her tablet (or phone). You'll see it in homes when kids are watching movies so their parents can find time to do chores or cook. And while there is nothing wrong with parents utilizing tools to give them time to attend to daily life chores, it is the things that kids are consuming that has become a greater source of concern.

On the surface, it may seem as if the content available to us (from YouTube to

Netflix) appears to be safe, especially with parent's trust on the rating system. But it is still essentially a very flawed system as demonstrated in research from the University of Pennsylvania's Annenberg Public Police Center that shows there is more gun violence in PG rated movies than R rated movies.

The media world constantly vies for our attention, eyeballs and pockets. This has led to a growing desensitization of audiences that has begun to create a distorted view of reality and aggressive behavior. By comparison, R rated films in the 1970s are very tame compared to PG versions of today's films.

At the same time, parents have found that banning children from media is not the solution either. Children will always find ways to consume media, whether through schools or at their friend's houses, so the question for Christian families still lingers, *"What can I do to make sure my child consumes the right kind of media?"*

This is why we've created Bible VR. The world of movies, TV and computer games has grown so large that it is all around us and we cannot ignore it. We wanted a safe alternative that is not only fun and educational, but one in which children can also learn more about the history of the Bible in a safe and non-hostile environment.

I started my foray into virtual reality during my tenure as a writer, producer and director of over 20 feature films in a 16-year period. Although VR really began in the 1960s, it was only recently that optical advances and pioneering inventors in the past six decades paved the way for low-cost and high quality devices. But it was really the advent of 360 cameras that birthed the idea of Bible VR beginning in 2012. Because virtual reality is still a very new technology, we are learning more and more every day about creating content for the Christian parent and/or student in order to provide them with tools to help them understand the Bible a little bit better.

It has been over 50 years since the Supreme Court decided in *Engel v. Vitale* that prayers were no longer allowed to be practiced in public schools and the Bible could no longer be taught. In the subsequent years, Christianity has experienced a sharp decline because fewer and fewer people are educated on the Bible in favor of secular sciences.

You do not see this problem in Israel, for example, because their faith is grounded in history and the environment around them. It would only make sense then, that Christians need to be exposed to the Holy Land and understand where historical events, miracles and stories of the Bible took place.

This would have been very cost prohibitive had it not been for the advent of virtual reality (VR) that has not only allowed for 360° immersive videos, but also transported the viewers straight into the Holy Land from the comfort of their own home.

Because VR is a relatively new technology in media, many people do not understand how to maximize its use. So, with this book I will not only shed some light into using and understanding VR, but how to use it properly.

VR, like any media, can be used for both good or bad. It is, therefore, important that we properly understand the tools at our disposal so that we can best utilize them. Give a man a hammer and he can pound on a nail, give that same hammer to a carpenter, and he can build you a table. It is my hope that this book can turn you into a 'carpenter'.

I want to thank you for taking on this exciting journey with me. As a student of learning, I hope that we can all discover this new and exciting world of VR together and utilize it to develop a greater understanding of the Bible, not only for ourselves, but to share with the rest of the world.

I pray everyday for the wisdom and knowledge to continue improving this new technology. I trust we can all pray that the Lord will guide us and provide us with the strength and confidence to enjoy this new technology.

Amen.

Dr. Pearry Teo, Ph.D, Min.D, Ed.D, CSC

What is Bible VR?

Virtual Reality (VR), defined by the Merriam-Webster dictionary is *an artificial environment which is experienced through sensory stimuli (such as sights and sounds) provided by a computer.* A person can experience virtual reality by connecting a headset to a computer and wearing it. With virtual reality, users can be transported into different worlds, play games or even explore the new emotions that come with such things as flying or even mountain bike riding.

A CHILD WEARING A VR HEADSET

WHAT THE CHILD IS ACTUALLY SEEING

There are many different kinds of VR devices on the market but they all perform the same simple function of *"put on VR headset: enter virtual world"* with the primary differences being cost and computing power. The current technology puts Oculus Rift and HTC Vive as the top VR headsets, but with a cost of a few hundred dollars and a powerful computing system, it is fairly inaccessible to many people. Conversely, Bible VR utilizes a creative way of tapping into your phone's computing power and through a downloadable app streams and delivers content to you from our servers, letting them do all the work. The cost for a headset to plug into your phone can be as cheap as USD$4.99 or a higher-end headset for around $79.99.

A PHONE CAN BE PLACED INTO A HEADSET TO EXPERIENCE VIRTUAL REALITY AT ANY PLACE.

BIBLE VR UTILIZES YOUR PHONE'S COMPUTING POWER TOGETHER WITH OUR SERVER SPEED TO STREAM TO YOU HUNDREDS OF CONTENT AT YOUR FINGERTIPS.

ALL YOU NEED IS TO DOWNLOAD THE APP TO BEGIN YOUR NEW EX-PERIENCES.

Bible VR is an app available on iOS and Android phones and is the first and largest collection of VR content created to be used specifically with the Bible. Once the app is on your phone, having Bible VR is like owning a little instant teleportation device to the Holy Land right at your fingertips, no matter where you may be.

There are many ways to use Bible VR:

- Visit the Holy Land to explore the holy sites in Israel where historical biblical events took place.

- Learn from professors of accredited Christian universities as they take you through these holy sites.

- Explore worlds such as Noah's Ark and learn about how it is possible to build one and how it would feel to be inside.

- Learn about the history of Israel, Egypt and Jordan.

- Visit Wonders of the World such as Petra and The Great Pyramids.

- and much more…

Bible VR can be used for those interested in exploring (tourism) and/or learning (education). VR has often times been used to help people being treated for emotional issues such as anxiety disorder. Being transported into holy places such as ancient churches or the top of Mount Sinai to experience a beautiful sunset has been shown to help reduce anxiety and create a perfect mental state for meditation.

In the end, it is how you use Bible VR that is more important than anything else. We have become so used to being force-fed content through media, that we often sit down and zone-out while we allow the transmitted entertainment to dull our minds into passivity. VR, on the other hand, is a very active media, so for those who do not like active experiences such as tourism or education, VR is not the right tool.

In this book, we will explore how to use Bible VR so that we can reap its benefits.

But like any benefit, one receives something by being an active participant in it. This is what makes VR special in that it asks for your engagement, whether through thinking or participation.

No one is going to learn by merely sitting down and staring at a TV screen. Even if you are learning something from a documentary, your mind has to be actively concentrating on the content, absorbing the information presented.

VR is a new way for people to learn, explore and experience new things through cutting edge technology. But there is a learning curve to everything, and often times, as it is with every new learning experience, it may come with its own little frustrations, so come along with me throughout this book and I will show you, step by step, how to experience VR as a new tool to learning more about the Bible and God.

FAMILIARIZING YOURSELF WITH VR

Before we continue with the book, it is a good idea to familiarize yourself with the app. We won't take a look at all its features, but just enough to get you started.

Don't be intimidated by the new technology and how it works right now. That's what this book is all about and more importantly than knowing how to use Bible VR is *why* you are using Bible VR.

So let's take a quick run through of the app so that you can better understand the context of what this book will talk about.

First of all, if you haven't already done so, download the Bible VR app available on the Apple iOS store or the Google Play store for your Android phone. Most newer model phones support VR playback so check that your phone is enabled for that. One quick way to check this is to Google your phone's model and see if it has a built-in gyroscope.

Once you've downloaded and launched the app, go ahead and sign-up so that the app can keep track of all your favorite VR videos and download them for offline use. It is very important in the sign-up process to make sure that you fill in your church's affiliation or ambassador's code (if you have one). This allows us to help contribute to your church or ambassador as all profits from the app go back to building the greater Kingdom of God.

Once you have successfully signed-up with us, there are two main ways you can experience Bible VR: one way is Bible VR mode, and the other is the VR Explorers mode. Don't worry, you will be

able to switch back and forth anytime later on. For this purpose, let's go to Bible mode, which is where your truest value really comes from!

You now have a very special Bible in your hands! As you can see, you can choose to find books of the Bible through it's traditional sorting or by alphabetical order. But what is special about this Bible is that you will see the little numbered icons on the side of each book. These numbered icons represent how many VR experiences are in the book. So, go ahead and let's click on *Genesis*.

WE ARE ALWAYS ADDING NEW CONTENT SO BE SURE TO UPDATE THE APP AND CHECK BACK OFTEN

Inside Genesis, you start off in chapter one. Of course, you can jump to any chapter by selecting a drop down menu at the top. As you see the list of chapters, you will see where the VR experiences are located, indicated by the little headset icon. Our list will be ever growing and we constantly add new experiences that you can view. Because we have one of the largest VR collections in the world, this is just one way we organize our library.

Now, let's go ahead and click on *Chapter 6*. In this particular chapter, the Bible talks about Noah's Ark. The VR experiences that we have accompanying this chapter include a VR exploration of an actual, life sized

Noah's Ark! By clicking on the icons below, you will get to step inside and see what it was really like. Go ahead and click on it! This whole series, like many others, is free.

If you clicked on the 'Play' button, the VR videos will play automatically. Clicking anywhere else in the icon will bring up a description for the video, allowing you to read more about it. When the video is playing, hold your phone in your hand and move it around. You will see that it tracks a whole 360° view of the entire place. You have absolute freedom to move and explore everything.

But what you are looking at right now is merely video mode, something for you to quickly preview it and see. For you to experience the real VR, click on the VR headset icon on the bottom of the video player that looks like this:

There will be instructions for you to insert your phone into a headset of your choice. You can easily find a headset of your liking and budget at popular retail places such as Amazon. They could range from prices as low as USD$4.99 to as high as USD$79.99.

As shown below, the VR experiences will then be shown in a 'split-eye' view and you should be able to experience it at the highest quality level depending on your internet speed. As with any server streaming services

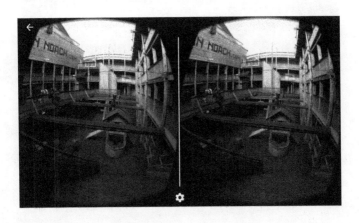

like Netflix, the quality of the video is dependent upon the speed of your internet. Because you are on your phone for this experience, be sure to remember to use an available WiFi connection so you are not incurring any additional data charges.

You have just successfully navigated the basics of Bible VR. Remember: you can always hit the back button at the top left hand corner of the screen and change the way you discover new faith based VR content.

As I mentioned before, another way to experience the VR content is through the VR Explorers section where footage is organized into categories as opposed to linking them through the Bible. While this may be a quicker way to find videos, the idea is that linking the Bible with its VR relevance is the core of Bible VR. You can take some time to navigate yourself around the VR Explorers but primarily, this book focuses on using Bible VR as part of your personal toolkit that helps you learn more about the Bible and the Kingdom of God.

Bible VR creates a heightened sense of what happens in and around the worlds of the Holy Land, as well as amplifying God's Word and how we all fit into the picture, historically and prophetically. VR is an empathy machine that enables you to not only see and hear things, but also to feel and experience them. Some people report slight dizziness after taking off the headsets as their mind must adjust back to being in the real world. Bible VR is a very engaging and immersive experience and the perfect tool to explore the worlds of the Bible.

What we experience, and how our minds learn things are all a part of the foundations of how we form our beliefs.

THE POWER OF BELIEF

Belief is arguably the most powerful and potent force in the universe. It is what binds us to our faith in God. It has also started every war fought throughout human history and is the very same force that creates the opposite emotion of love. It is responsible for all facets of religion and science. Science also approaches any examination of the world and the universe with a firm belief in its own preconceived notions. After all, man has to have a belief – or at least a sense of wonder - that something is real or possible before he turns that hypothesis into facts.

The reason I am dedicating a whole chapter to the power of belief is to underscore the importance of understanding how much the emotion of belief plays a much larger role in the creation of the learning and grounding of your knowledge of the Bible.

"These things are written so that you may know what you believe..."

1 John 5:13

We know belief is important. The Bible talks about it everywhere. From David's belief that with God's help he would be able to defeat Goliath, to the resurrection of Jesus, belief plays one of the most important roles in the Bible. It enables shepherds to become kings, kings to create empires, prophets to perform miracles and people to receive blessings.

In the secular world, belief is equally important. It has given men power of creation, good or evil. Belief influences our minds in certain manners that drive behavior. Behind every action, decision and communication are beliefs. It can inspire life and death, and it has also helped ordinary people do extraordinary things.

While ordinary people, despite the evidence, neglect the strength of what belief can do, marketing and politics have been capitalizing on it for years. By manipulating our beliefs, they can mold and shape the world to any form they want.

HOW MEDIA INFLUENCES US

If you have ever watched a movie, listened to music or read a book and become so 'swept away' to another world, or empathized so much with a character that you feel happiness for their success, or heartbreak for their misfortune, then you are not alone. You are experiencing a phenomenon known as **narrative transportation.**

Narrative transportation is a psychological phenomenon where people who lose themselves in a story carry influences that affect their attitudes, intentions and behaviors into real life, even when the film or book is over. It is a powerful experience that can change how we see the world. It has the ability to instill beliefs in us that can inspire great things or horrible outcomes. Could *The Pursuit of Happyness* inspire a legion of people to overcome difficulties by taking action? Could *The Dark Knight* have inspired a man to dress as The Joker and massacre people in a movie theater?

While it is the responsibility of content creators (musicians, film directors, writers) to create positive influences on the audiences' experience, it is incumbent upon us all to take notice of trends in current secular entertainment and take a long look as to where it is heading these days. Films and novels are getting more and more violent in order to appease a desensitized public, while music preaches more about sex than love and all sorts of other entertainment media have become more hardened, crass and demoralizing in their delivery. I urge you to start looking around, develop your vision and begin observing these trends with your very own eyes.

While the Bible contains many stories that give us narrative transportation (rooting for the underdog David as he battles with Goliath), secular media has largely taken over because stories are devolving to remain relevant to the public's changing tastes as they become more desensitized to violence, graphic action and lustful experiences. The Bible itself is filled and rife with stories of lust, violence and graphic depictions of events, but it is still, primarily, a collected anthology of books written for the purpose of establishing belief and furthering faith tradition. We cannot change these stories nor fit them into the narrative worlds, but we can help our kids to experience the narrative transportation of the Bible first, before their minds become desensitized by today's media.

I am not talking just about R rated movies, I am also talking about cartoons and other animated features. Cartoons go for bigger magical experiences and alien creatures. The top three grossing animated films in recent history are Frozen (using magic), Minions (cute aliens) and Toy Story 3 (toys coming to life). On the surface they may appear to be innocent movies, but there are darker stakes at play.

Dr. Sarah Coyne from Brigham Young University and author of *Child Development* conducted a study with preschool children in which she demonstrated that a child's perception of femininity, drawn from these tv shows and animated films, affects their beliefs and development later in life. Little girls grow up to believe in what the media decides would be ideals of beauty, and in essence, the media slowly begins to control our patterns of belief, starting at a very young age.

LEARNING NEGATIVE BEHAVIORS

Knowing that our consumption of media shapes our beliefs at a very young age, let's go deeper and see how these beliefs can shape the behaviors that completely determine how a person grows up.

There was a study by Joslin, Fletcher and Emlen in 1964 that studied two different types of monkeys. They compared the fear responses of a wild-reared monkey and a lab-reared monkey and found out that only the wild-reared monkey had a fear of snakes.

While it is natural to fear snakes due to survival instincts (especially in the wild), the study goes further to determine how these wild-reared monkeys learn to be fearful of a creature that could pose a potential threat to its survival. And they found:

Wild monkeys learned to fear the threat of snakes by observing other monkeys.

To test this hypothesis, they exposed the lab-reared monkey to a wild-reared monkey.

They watched as the lab-reared monkey observed the wild-reared monkey when it encountered a snake and displayed fear responses. The lab-reared monkey very quickly learned to be afraid of snakes too, even though the snake had never caused any harm to it. This indicates how outside influence can shape our beliefs about certain things.

But I left one thing out:

The lab-reared monkeys learned how to have a fear of snakes by watching a _video_ of another monkey.

That is the power of what media can do to living beings. It can help shape our beliefs and create positive or negative influences in our lives. But you could be saying "But these are monkeys, humans know what is real and fake in the media!"

But it does happen to humans as well. The movie *Jaws* has been credited for creating shark phobias, which was a study conducted by Ali Mattu and James Hambrick of the Columbia University Clinic for Anxiety and Related Disorders. Although statistics show that dying as a result of a shark attack is one-in-3.7-million (according to National Geographic), this did not stop many nervous beachgoers from developing a fear of shark attacks.

Again, when you begin to understand the nature of how media can influence our beliefs, you will start to see it become very obvious in your observations.

When you start to understand this behavioral pattern, you begin to see how media can also influence the way people perceive God, religion and even Christianity. Movies like *The Mist, Red State, Silent Hill, The Godfather, The Village* and even *The Matrix*, promote in a very subtle way that people who place their belief in something unseen are often ignorant and blind. But yet, there are many things we cannot see that we know exist. Love and inspiration are a couple of examples. We may not see love and inspiration, but we see the effects of them around us. Same as with our belief in God. But with media influencing our beliefs, no amount of facts may be able to reverse the damage.

Other damaging traits exist that seek to tackle our social construct, rather than directly attacking God, in order to denounce religion. A movie like *Footloose* (an '80s classic), utilizes one of its main characters to promote the idea that religious people are filled with smug self-righteousness. Documentary filmmakers, Rachel Grady and Heidi Ewing, filmed *Jesus Camp* to infer that Christians are all unintelligent extremists. Every religious person is hideous looking and dies horrible excruciating deaths in *The Name of The Rose*. Priestly abuse is shown in harrowing detail in films such as *The Magdalene Sisters, The Boys of St. Vincent* and many others. You begin to see how media portrays Christians and their beliefs as being no longer socially acceptable in the secular world. This is why the younger generation, with easier access to media, begins to see religion as both a questionable, moral and social liability. Even if you present the facts to them, you cannot change their core belief once it is formed.

THE INTERNET

The internet was created to be an information portal that has become a part of our society and culture. More than three billion people are using the internet, right now, and for almost everybody, the internet has become a source for garnering information, learning and even consuming media.

If we understand that the media we consume creates our beliefs, we can then understand why the internet has created an existential crisis for many people due to its promotion of unchecked free speech and fake news. When the lines between what is real and what is fake become blurred, people are creating and holding on to beliefs that may not only be false, but also damaging to them psychologically and, more importantly, spiritually.

In the previous segment, I presented to you a list of movies that I said promotes the ideology of people believing in something they cannot see as being ignorant and blind. You may have noticed I put the film *The Godfather* in there. Chances are, you did not stop to critically think of how I arrived at that conclusion. But by me giving several true and real narratives, and putting in one false narrative, I can change the way people perceive something, albeit true or not.

This is how the internet works.

If beliefs are formed by our observations of reality (or pseudo reality) together with our judgment skills, then the internet distorts all of that. The data on the internet is a series of algorithms aimed at curating content to suit our preferences, interests and personality while enhancing existing biases and undermining our motivation to learn new things.

These search engines, news aggregators and feed rankings perpetuate an ignorance rather than knowledge. The rise of social media like Twitter, Facebook and Instagram intensifies feelings of loneliness and ideological isolation. Think about people who use social media to 'connect,' but end up gluing their faces to the screen instead of meeting people face-to-face. The false belief that social media is making a person more connected shows how easily the internet can be used to sway the minds of youth in our society.

The rise in social media in forming our beliefs not only utilizes the powerful tools of algorithms, but they also utilize the power of relationships to enhance these false beliefs. Consider that fake news stories have more engagement than 19 of the main news outlets combined. The popularity of the unwitting spread of false belief is due to social media like Facebook. Because a 'friend' is sharing the fake news, you automatically give some credibility to those stories or facts because they have come from what we consider to be a reliable source (a friend or family member). Your brain links up those two things to create a new false belief around a perceived true narrative.

A fake 2018 news story stating that Pope Francis was cancelling the Bible and proposing a new Holy Book spread like wild fire all over social media, mostly due to the sharing of news feeds. This distortion of information works deep into our core beliefs and perceptions and further reinforces these false narratives resulting in a phenomenon known as echo chambers.

ECHO CHAMBERS

An echo chamber (an epistemic bubble) is a metaphorical description of a situation where social structures use cherry picked information enhanced with communication and repetition to create false beliefs and narratives. Different intellectual communities no longer share the same basic foundational beliefs as nobody knows how to discern what is true in the world of the internet anymore.

An echo chamber, specifically, is a social structure where other relevant voices have been actively discredited. This is why you will find science constantly discrediting religion (despite the fact that there is enough evidence to indicate that science and religion are actually quite complementary). This is why you will find people sharing more and more information about science rather than faith based issues.

This phenomenon is further enhanced through social media sharing sites. As a person (reading from his friend's feed) begins to believe in other narratives because of consistent and repetitive one-sided information, you begin to find said person developing these beliefs based upon social constructs and fake news.

Echo chambers create biased information. How are we to form healthy beliefs regarding the information we receive if our observations of the world are viewed through biased lenses?

You begin to see how beliefs work, and how it could potentially be damaging especially with how culture and media have such immense power to influence our thinking. What can be done about it?

It is far easier to let someone else do the job. Why not just relax in the atmosphere of entertainment and fun with family and friends when is it so much more work to develop and foster healthy beliefs? It is because it's far easier to enjoy the fruits of consumption, rather than to be responsible decipherers of fact. We consume media and technology because we believe it makes life easier and more entertaining. We already believe that high schools and colleges are filled with what we would consider to be 'worldly' music, addictive substances, alcohol, drugs, devilish dancing, sensual women, lustful men and other things we would consider to be ungodly. We also know that people enjoy these hedonistic pleasures because we possess a false, ingrained belief that consumption is good.

And the opposite of consumption is production. God never intended for us to be consumers alone, he intended for us to be producers. Tools are given to us to be producers and using those tools wisely is where real blessings can happen. So let's explore what VR can do for creating healthy beliefs.

Those who work their land will have abundant good, but those who chase fantasies have no sense."
Proverbs 12:11

THE EMPATHY MACHINE

Empathy is the ability to understand, appropriate and share the feelings of another. It is undoubtedly one of the core tenets of Christianity around the world.

Share each other's burdens, and in this way obey the law of Christ. If you think you are too important to help someone, you are only fooling yourself. You are not that important."

Galatians 6:2-3

Now there is a difference between empathy and sympathy. While they both share the same roots of the Greek term *páthos* meaning "suffering, feeling," the prefix *sym-* comes from the Greek term meaning "with, together with" and the *em-* meaning "within, in." The difference being that with sympathy you are feeling compassion, sorrow or pity for the hardships of another, while empathy is understanding what the other person is encountering by putting yourself in the shoes of another.

VR is the ultimate empathy machine because for the first time, you can literally "put on the shoes of another." By wearing the VR headset, you immediately feel as though you are transported into another time and another place, where the Biblical events happened in real history.

Imagine standing in the exact spot where Jesus was born, or where he was baptized or crucified. Stand at the top of Mount Sinai where Moses met face-to-face with God, and many other places. Suddenly, the Bible feels less of a book of stories and morals, but rather *an experience*.

Don't worry about experiencing VR and wondering what's next and what you are doing at these different places. The worlds of the Bible are so vast that the first time entering them through Bible VR you may feel lost about what to do, or how to feel. It is like the first time anyone sees the intimidating structure of the Bible and how enormous it truly is. We are going to take this experience slowly. But for the purpose of this book, I want you to understand exactly what VR is doing or can do to you.

The ultimate benefit of VR as a tool is what you get out of it, rather than what the latest technology and content may be.

Before undertaking any VR experience, try to understand, first, precisely why you are watching it. What are you trying to empathize and learn? Using Bible VR as your empathy machine to try and understand the worlds of the Bible does more than just explore the Bible, it can also change you as a person.

EMPATHY BENEFITS

Empathy is one of the greatest interpersonal tools a person can develop. Empathy not only makes you compassionate, but unlike sympathy, helps you develop skills you use everyday as a believing Christian.

With empathy you will:

- treat the people you care about in the manner *they* want to be treated, rather than how *you* want to be treated.

- understand the needs of those around you at home, church and work.

- have less trouble dealing with problems both at home and at work.

- learn how to motivate and inspire those around you.

- effectively share the message of The Good Book without being aggressive.

- lower your personal stress levels

- help all your relationships by creating a feeling of connectedness to one another
- make you and everyone around you into better leaders

VR's connection to empathy is heightened because we are, for the first time, able to share experiences within close proximity. But it takes time, so be patient with yourself as you are using Bible VR. Remember that in most of us, our minds are constantly fighting us. While entering a VR simulation and being in another culture, there is also that lingering, logical part of your brain telling you that this isn't real. Effectively, you step back and begin to see the whole experience as fictional, or 'just a video'.

For most people, it can take a few attempts, sometimes taking even a few weeks to a month to really start getting the hang of it. To diminish all bias takes work. But as I said before, consuming healthy media isn't going to be easy. But the benefits are clearly there for us!

WHO EMPATHY IS FOR

Not everybody who uses VR will automatically begin to develop empathetic qualities. The bottom line is that you *have to be sincere about wanting to be empathetic.* No amount of awe, technology or the 'cool factor' can persuade anybody of how amazing the world of the Bible is to experience. They have to be open to that experience for themselves, first.

This is why I have emphasized that before beginning a VR experience, it is crucial to understand the context of that world you are about to enter.

By way of example, take the Bible VR experience of *Golgotha* in *The Church of The Holy Sepulchre.* A secular person who first puts on a headset and is transported to the location where Jesus was crucified would immediately pass it off as a beautiful, artistically detailed church structure built around a so-called 'holy site.' That person will then walk away with nothing more intimate than somebody who merely views architecture for the sake of viewing architecture. The scenery could almost bore him.

A Christian experiencing the VR might take a little bit more from it and appreciate being able to visit such a holy place and may even find greater meaning in the spectacle behind this amazing church. They will begin to feel that the story of Jesus' crucifixion is no longer just words in a book, but an experience shared together with the rest of the world. Their faith is now bolstered, not only in the belief in the Biblical story, but rather, their experience of being in the world of the Bible, seeing it, hearing it, sensing it.

An empathetic Christian will be the person who takes away the most from the experience by observing the culture around them. Smack dab in the middle of Old City

Jerusalem, they will notice and begin to realize that the impact of Jesus extends so much further than they once realized to Protestant and Catholic alike. They will see Muslims in hijabs and taqiyahs come to pay respect to Jesus and begin to appreciate the impact that such an important historical figure has made on the world. They will learn, through doing some external digging later on, that even the Islamic holy text, the *Quran*, mentions Jesus (*Isa ibn Maryam* - Jesus Son of Mary) 25 times, born of the virgin Mary (19:30:21) and whom also refers to him as *run min Allah* (Spirit of God), *mushier bi'l baraka* (The Messiah), *kalimah min Allah* (Word from/of God), and *rasul* (Prophet-Messenger) of God.

The empathetic Christian sees his faith suddenly coming together with the rest of the world, while others only see the differences in other religious belief systems.

This is especially powerful because the VR experience transcends common perceptions, revealing a much more harmonious world of rhythm, symmetry and equality. One would never know this unless they step into and share the same world, prayers and respect of the same locations with different people in different countries. Short of going there yourself, VR not only transports you there, but gives you the ability to go there anytime you want.

Remember, our current world of religious strife is only a product of media perpetuating our erroneous beliefs. For them, fear and violence is what sells the news and keeps your eyes glued to the screen. Counter to what the media has you believing, the world is much more at peace (except for the one percent of psychopaths) than you might comprehend at the hands of the media.

This is how empathy can chip away at old systems of belief and start to build and reinforce healthy beliefs to replace them. VR is a tool that can be used successfully to help foster and spread empathy to everyone around the world. No longer are you a slave to what the media tells you. With Bible VR, you can now go there, unrestricted and uncensored.

Roman Krznaric writes amazing books on empathy that can be useful reads. In them, he identifies the habits of highly empathetic people as being able to:

- Cultivate curiosity about strangers
- Challenge prejudices and discover commonalities
- Try another person's life
- Listen hard and open up
- Inspire mass action and social change
- Develop an ambitious imagination

These traits alone paint a very striking portrait of a powerful Christian. It also displays the attributes of Jesus Christ when he walked on this earth.

USING EMPATHY TO GROW

We created Bible VR to be a tool. It is not something in which someone will simply hand the information over to you. It was designed and built for you to observe and experience the Holy Land and to open up your appreciation of our beautiful word and faith. While Bible VR provides you with some historical, archaeological and geographical information, it is in your personal stand-alone experience that the real, potential power dwells. And this is because VR has to be *YOUR* personal experience. The good in VR is not in what we offer you, but what you get out of it. If you do not want to grow or care about the Holy Land, no amount of fancy film shooting, or awe-inspiring landscape is going to change your mind or beliefs. You have to *want it* as a Christian.

With VR, you can have a collective experience not only with other Christians, but also with the peoples of the other Abrahamic religions (Judaism and Islam). You'll learn how we all came from the same history and the same Holy Writs. And you'll also learn more about your history as a

Christian. Holy sites are extremely important to your foundations as a Christian, because it grounds you to your faith. Remember, you are no longer just reading the Word, you are experiencing it where it all happened. These are not stories, but actual events that took place.

How were times different back then? How do they affect social and cultural changes today? These are the great questions for the growing empathetic Christian. You want to know more about the Bible because it turns blind faith into belief and legitimate belief into knowing. It is one thing to read stories, it is another thing to stand on the spot and experience it where it actually happened. You can then share it with your family and share it with the world. VR has changed the landscape in that we are no longer limited to physical travel anymore!

You can experience total immersion from the comfort of your home.

For everything created by God is good, and nothing is to be rejected if it is received with thanksgiving, for it is made holy by the word of God and prayer. If you put these things before the brothers, you will be a good servant of Christ Jesus, being trained in the words of the faith and of the good doctrine that you have followed."

1 Timothy 4:4-6

VR IMMERSION

Practice these things, immerse yourself in them, so that all may see your progress."
1 Timothy 4:15

The five major milestones in the gospel narrative of the life of Jesus are his baptism, transfiguration, crucifixion, resurrection and ascension. Christians all over the world perform baptism by immersion (based on the transliteration rather than the actual translation of the Koine Greek word, "baptidzo," which literally means "immersion") to commemorate their symbolic action of recognizing that Jesus died for our sins. Immersion is an important symbolic meaning for us all, as the first act of cognitive obedience in a believing Christian.

It should be noted that like all good Christians, practicing faith shouldn't end on

Sunday or after baptism. Believing Christians should always seek ways to continually immerse themselves with the teachings of the Bible in order to build our faith and relationship with God.

Immersing yourself in the Christian lifestyle by trusting in Him and keeping His commandments are just part of our ever growing relationship with God. But following God with blind faith alone creates a rocky foundation from which we can be easily seduced away, broken upon or tempted by the secular world. As we explore finding ways we can further strengthen this personal relationship with God through Jesus, as well as finding effective tools to assist us, Bible VR becomes just one answer. To understand how immersive tools contribute to your relationship with God, we will dedicate one entire chapter to this.

There are many ways we strengthen our relationship with God. From prayer and mediation or fellowshipping with other believers in church, we strive to not only spend time in the presence of God, but to also learn more about him through pastors, priests and other clergy. We know that one of the best investments we can make in our lives is in the fostering of strong, healthy relationships with those we love, and this includes, most importantly, our relationship with God.

How can VR help with your relationship? By providing a safe immersive environment to feel grateful and affected by the Kingdom of God. We see the Holy Land and who it was that God chose to be 'His People.' We can also empathize with them when he chose Israel and freed them from Egypt. In the past, it would be difficult to explain how all of these things could change the way you see the Holy Land, especially if you had never been there. But with VR, that can all change.

There are many modes and methods available today to learn about the Bible. Apart from actually reading the Bible, there are countless books, movies, videos, documentaries, apps and additional reading materials available today. Where Bible VR stands apart is it now introduces immersive experience into the mix. When immersed in a VR world, you are no longer just absorbing information, you are experiencing it.

This is where things start to get interesting...

CREATING YOUR REALITY

Remember we talked about belief and how it is the most potent force in the universe? Your life is a direct reflection of your belief structure. Christians live their lives in accordance to the mandates, teachings and commandments found in the Bible, while a secular person creates their own belief structure through observation of their environment, which can be very unstable in this modern age. These belief structures then create a 'collective reality' in which people's actions and patterns of living are a direct result of the power of their belief. How many Christians have reported their life changing 180 degrees once they have accepted Lord Jesus Christ into their hearts. You can hear the personal testimonies in your church, but all over the internet you can read about some truly amazing stories where lives have been turned around.

But that doesn't mean that it stops right there for Christians. We continue to grow every day by building our relationship with God. We do it by strengthening our beliefs every day.

So what creates belief?

Belief is created by the sum of your experiences. Without experiences, it is merely faith - faith in God, faith in Jesus, etc., etc., etc. This happens when you have no experience with the Divine and you are living your life on blind faith alone. This is why it is very hard to convert a secular person to Christianity, unless he or she has had some divine experiences that accompany their faith. Blind faith is something that is almost too big to hope for in today's world dominated by science and hard facts.

This is why we believed Bible VR was so important when we created it. Virtual reality helps create these simulated environments where you can experience God's Holy Kingdom. By *experiencing* it, rather than seeing, hearing or just reading about it, you begin to turn your faith into a strong, rooted belief. I call this *grounding your faith*.

360° IMMERSION

VR experiences are not like 3D movies at all. They not only seem real or pop out to you, they actually make you feel like you are in that place. If a photo is worth a thousand words, how many words is a video worth, and then how many words is a VR experience worth?

I couldn't tell you. As mentioned before, as people, we are a collection of our experiences. They shape our beliefs and make our reality. How you feel about immersing yourself in God's kingdom is primarily based upon your relationship with him and your current belief sets. Everybody is different.

360-degree videos are essentially like personal field trips. And having a library accessible in your phone is like being able to take any of your friends along on those field trips. Who would have thought a year ago that you could say "Hey, want to go to the Valley of Elah where David and Goliath fought?" This immersion not only creates new experiences as you are able to observe these places freely and unencumbered, but it can also augment your sharing of the Good Word with a friend, raising the level of engagement.

360-degree videos help you make better connections with your learning. It provides concrete visual explanations for you by putting you directly into this world. The Bible is no longer a book you read about and then imagine what it is like, but it is now a book you can read and then experience. This is made easier when you use the online Bible in the Bible VR app and as you are reading your chapters and verses, you will be notified when there is a VR experience that goes along with the content.

When you are present in a location or watching an event happen, you are introducing a sense of presence within as you begin to marry yourself into the word of the Bible. This interaction not only has the potential of developing greater empathy and deeper understanding, but it also grounds you into what is real and leaves you *knowing* that it is real.

By being at these places in VR, you will find that you begin to develop a capacity to enhance your understanding of the Bible's historical context, geographical settings and moral attributes. Pastors who have effectively used Bible VR in their sermons take their congregation to places they could never have gone before. Imagine what it would be like to not only listen to your pastor's sermons about prayer, but to also learn it with your pastor while you are actually in the Garden of Gethsemane where Jesus prayed.

Now, this is education on a whole new level!

DISADVANTAGES OF VR IMMERSION

VR immersion is not for everybody. For some, it could be intense and engaging, but the opposite side of the spectrum works too. Because VR immersion is so new, many people will approach the technology and will leave feeling confused and bored. But that is what this book is all about!

If you notice, our VR experiences are limited to only a few minutes each. Unlike traditional videos where people can spend hours glued to a particular scene, VR

Immersion is very brief in comparison, yet extremely intense, so we limit each of these experiences to a few minutes to give people the time to recalibrate their orientation back to the present world. It is also a time, if you're around family and friends, to discuss your own personal experiences and share whatever you learn or discover with them.

The introduction of VR is akin to the introduction of common core mathematics. When first introduced, it changed the way math problems were tackled and it frustrated a lot of parents who were used to tackling problems the old, traditional way. In the past, getting the right answer to a math problem was the goal, but today, common core mathematics focuses on the importance for students to understand the principles behind the mathematical problem. This is a foreign concept to many people.

For example, the old technique in solving the problem of '10,000 divided by 100' was to eliminate the additional zeroes. While the answer is the same, the students utilize 'bags of tricks' to solve the problem as opposed to really thinking about the question. While there is always a shortcut to thinking, it is in the understanding of the root of questions - the *why* rather than the *how* - that moves VR immersion from the category of entertainment into critical thinking and knowledge.

VR immersion also does not work for people who see VR as a very private experience. Because it is a technology based upon personal experience, those who look upon Christianity as a tool for social gatherings and friends may initially find VR to be a very lonely experience. Although we will discuss later how VR can be used as a socially enriching tool - especially for the family - initial thoughts on VR can leave a bad taste in a person's mouth if they are not adequately prepared to personally appropriate such a vastly new technology. This is partially caused by the rise in social networking and media, which decreases face-to-face relationships, and is linked to the significant decrease in empathy amongst young people. As I mentioned earlier, what one may view as a networking tool may actually be working as an opposite against their beliefs.

One of the greatest disadvantages of 360-degree video is the deconstruction of illusion. Many people may be shocked to see that holy sites around the world are not what they imagined in their mind's eye. The allure of the fantasies created in our minds is always much brighter, more vivid and better than what we end up actually experiencing in reality, because the experience is created personally, so there is a vested interest in this illusion of fantasy. This was certainly different to the Israelites who entered the promised land, in that while it was no paradise, it was a *"good and spacious land, a land flowing with milk and honey"* (Exodus. 3:8).

For example, many people assume the battlefield in which David and Goliath fought is set atop an epic landscape of mountains in the desert where armies would gather in ranks to the beating sounds of drums as one of the most legendary and heroic standoffs in history ensued. However, a look at the VR experience filmed in the Valley of Elah shows smaller, low mountain ranges covered in lush grasses, honking cars passing by the freeway beyond them destroys the illusion of a great battle that has been painted in our minds. While we want to show off the magnificence of the Bible, it is more important that we show the reality, where things happened in real history, without censorship, without trying to paint more glorious portraits or cater to a more desensitized public that needs and craves the increasingly more necessary grandiose. The effect of being at this historical place is largely up to the viewer to discern its importance rather than sugar coating the experience. God did not provide a fleet of transportation vehicles for the Israelites when they were freed from Egypt and setting out on their 40 year nomadic journey. The journey, however difficult it may seem at the onset, is what you make of it.

As you continue your journey on your ever-increasing quest for knowledge and understanding, always remember that how you utilize the Bible VR tool is more important than understanding its physical function. A hammer is nothing to a fisherman, and a fishing rod is nothing to a carpenter. Give the right people the right tools and you will see them produce rather than simply consume.

A NEW TOOL

What you get out of Bible VR is solely up to you as an individual. To immerse yourself in the Holy Land, God's promised land to Israel, can be nothing short of spectacular. But be warned, your approach to it and your mindset about its efficacy is completely within your making. Bible VR, while a vibrant tool, can also be an incredibly dull experience, solely based upon how you approach its use. It is up to you to decide the reason for using Bible VR as a tool, rather than making it a means to an end.

A person who is filled with the Holy Spirit can be likened to the state of being drunk. In the Apostle Paul's letter to the Ephesians, he says that being filled with the Spirt is so much better than being "drunk with wine." But he also makes a sideways comparison between the Spirit and spirits, in that wine or alcohol can consume your life, just as the Holy Spirit can be all-consuming. Being "drunk with the Holy Spirit" means you are controlled and consumed by the Holy Spirit of God that dwells within you, filling your life and helping you to live a holy life.

Those who are drunk with the Holy Spirit live their lives through the commandments of their heavenly father. Exploring Bible VR and the holy sites in Israel is akin to visiting your spiritual, ancestral home. Israel is God's promised land to Jacob and all the descendants of Abraham, as shown in Genesis 28:13.

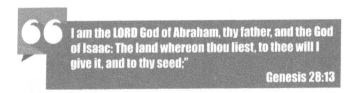

I am the LORD God of Abraham, thy father, and the God of Isaac: The land whereon thou liest, to thee will I give it, and to thy seed;"

Genesis 28:13

Now I am not inferring that one has to be filled with The Holy Spirit to appreciate

Bible VR. Every Christian is on a different, personal path in their development to a closer relationship with God. Being on different paths does not make one Christian better than another. It is completely erroneous and antithetical to the Christian walk to feel that just because one has a greater knowledge of the Bible they are granted some sort of special right to claim a higher social status within God's Kingdom.

Quite the opposite.

God's purpose for us in our individual lives can manifest in very different ways for each individual. My personal journey has surely been a unique one and I'd be surprised to find another person in this world who has travelled the same journey and created the same relationship with God as I have. When looking at whether one can use Bible VR as a tool for their spiritual journey, one only has to pray and ask for guidance. *"If any of you lacks wisdom, ask of God who gives to all, liberally and without holding back,"* so said the Apostle in James 1:5.

Perhaps, at this point in your life, there are bigger, more important things for you to learn before endeavoring into the deeper history of the promised land.

That's what Bible VR is. On a surface level it is a tool that Christians all over the world can use to visit the promised land. However, for many Christians around the world, it is used as a tool to gain a deeper understanding about the promised land itself.

Why is the promised land, the Holy Land, so important for Christians? Biblically speaking, it is a tangible reminder that God keeps his promises. Prophets in the Bible have foretold that the nations of the world would work to thwart the will of God in this matter. One only needs to Google the latest news of Israel to see how this is happening RIGHT NOW.

The political strife that takes place within God's promised land should not by any means take away any Christian's right to visit it. My trips to Israel have been nothing short of life changing and while I am blessed by God to have the opportunity, this opportunity is limited to many others, not only for the dangers birthed in religious and political strife, but financial limitations as well.

For a foreigner to visit Israel, vast amounts of money must be spent. From airplane tickets, to hotels, food, land transportation and spending money. A week's trip to Israel can easily be a USD $4,000 (per person) venture, and this does not include anything I would purchase such as souvenirs or personal trinkets.

The idea for creating Bible VR came when I had the dream of being able to visit God's promised land any time I wished, and my prayers were answered in the new technology of Bible VR. In this chapter, let us explore the different ways we can use this innovative tool to learn more about the original promise of God.

RIGHT TOOLS, RIGHT TIME

The best way to effectively use our tools is to incorporate them at the right time and for the right reasons. Many people keep a hammer in their house in case they may need it. They do not use a hammer for every repair job, despite it being a common household tool, but they keep one around for when the occasion rises for its use

Bible VR is similar in that it is not necessary to use it all the time. But knowing *when* to use it is fundamental to enriching each experience you have. This is why the easiest way to use Bible VR is when you are reading the Bible. The VR experiences linked inside the Bible VR mode helps you enhance your Bible reading and prayer sessions. You could simply read the Bible at your own pace, for reflection and study and utilize the VR experiences as they appear, as enhancements to your personal devotions. Don't make the mistake of trying to experience everything all at once. Pacing yourself will give you the most rewarding experience, as you will then have the time to reflect on each one individually.

The VR Explorer's menu has been designed for quicker access to VR experiences. But they were never meant to be viewed as the primary method for experiencing the Bible. It is best used if you want to discuss or revisit certain VR locations, whether you are talking with friends or family or simply want to pull it up quickly. Ultimately, we designed Bible VR so that you can complement your readings of the Bible.

But where do you start? Sometimes the thought of opening the Bible can be very intimidating due to its size, diverse information and the finding of relevant materials for your everyday life and your own knowledge or academic pursuits. Remember, the Bible is filled with information ranging from history, to prophecy to poetry to the art of daily living. You do not have to start from Genesis 1:1! Most people start with The Gospel of John, where the book gives you a good understanding of who Jesus is and what his ministry is about. You'll find that we have also focused a lot of our VR content in The Gospels. Where you start depends on your personal goals. Some may choose to pray and let the Lord guide them to a verse or passage, while many rely on the sermons of their pastors to guide them.

THE WHOLE STORY

The Bible is filled with many different stories and accounts. Some are more narrative centric, such as David and Goliath, Jonah and the Big Fish, Jesus turning the water into wine or The Ten Plagues. Often times, we read about more character centric stories as we look into the lives of prophets and people such as Abraham, Solomon, or Paul. From there, we learn about stories through morals, journeys and redemptive tales while also learning about God's love and revelations of his purpose for humanity.

If there is a VR experience linked together with the story, finish the story first. It is then best to use the VR to reflect on those stories. Imagine if you were to read the story of Noah's Ark for yourself or your kids and then being able to transport yourself into that world. Use that time to reflect upon those stories. Rather than doing it in your imagination while sitting in your room or a Bible study group, why not reflect on it in the actual places where it happened? This creates that grounding effect we spoke about earlier, enabling you to see, hear and reflect upon your scripture readings.

Bloom's Taxonomy suggests that pupils remember 90% of things they say and do. VR experiences help with that as you can not only experience it, you can also review it later with your friends or family and open up a discussion about what each other got out of their own personal experiences with it.

LOOKING FOR JESUS

The stories and characters in the Bible, while authored by many different people, all have in their divine inspiration, a much bigger, deeply richer thematic purpose, and that is the Messiah and Kinsman Redeemer, Jesus. Not only is he central to the theme of the redemption of mankind that permeates the scriptures, but every plot line, every moral and every teaching can find its root or its intention pointing forward or hailing back to Jesus. Start your exploration by seeking his character, his values and his teachings all within the stories in the Bible, then, when you experience the VR locations in Bible VR, look around as you begin to find his message everywhere.

You can look a the VR experiences in Bible VR as meditative locations where you can sit down, see where it all happened, and use those moments to truly reflect on the Bible's message. The great benefit of personal reflection in Bible VR is to consider that even when you are in Israel as part of a tour group, you would not be given the chance to sit and personally reflect on your own as each group has to move at a very quick pace to cover even a small percentage of the locations you are visiting in a single day.

Bible VR gives you unlimited time to reflect upon the Bible, paying off a thousand-fold over its value.

DISCOVER, LEARN, EXPLORE

Bible VR has different ways in which you can obtain the richest experience. You will see that we classify our VR experiences inside Bible VR as *Learn*, *Explore*, and *Discover*.

Learn VR experiences centralize around Biblical scholar Dr. Tim Laniak, who is the dean of old testament studies in the prestigious Gordon Conwell Seminary School. He provides a walkthrough at the Biblical sites demonstrating how they relate to scripture. Dr. Tim Laniak approaches this from an educational point of view and is best for those who want to 'learn more about it' on an academic level.

Discover VR experiences follow *Trip Advisor's* award-winning tour guide, Danny the Digger, as he takes you around the Holy Land and shows you the rich history of the promised land through geography and archaeology. A well-known archaeologist himself, Danny's approach is on a more friendly level, catering to the tourist who wants to explore the Holy Land without any deep religious background.

Explore VR experiences are the core of what Bible VR is all about. On the surface, they just appear to be VR experiences without a teacher or tour guide, but they were meant to be used in a much more elaborate way, augmenting your personal time with God. We will discuss more about meditation in the following chapters but understand that *Explore* VR experiences were created to be at the heart of your personal time with God.

Bible VR was created for you to use as exciting new ammunition for your spiritual warfare and journey. The key is always to know when to use the right tools at the right time. You do not have to try and do everything all at once. Take it little by little and over time, you will begin to see the difference it can make in your personal devotions to God.

ESCAPE FROM THE WORLD

We are constantly in a world full of noise. Whether you are at work or home, we are living in a room full of the noises of everyday life. Escapism is nothing new. People have turned to the TV, internet and smartphones to escape from the world that perpetually buzzes around them. But as marketers become privy to what our eyes are viewing and where our interests take us, they begin to dominate markets once used for escapism as a tool for advertising and belief control.

We designed Bible VR to be a true escape away from the noise of the world; an emotionally healthy way for you to escape for brief periods of time. Part of the allure of virtual reality and the contents of Bible

VR is the shorter times of immersion. By keeping content short, we can find some escape from the noise in the world without turning into an avoidance form of living.

This is why television series and computer games hold such a dominant position in our society. People may use these things to escape from the world, but the high level of time investment in these media can slowly turn people into media addicts, sometimes causing them to avoid life's duties. There are many therapies for computer game addiction, which is now officially classified as a mental health disorder by the WHO (World Health Organization) in their 2018 International Classification of Diseases.

So the question is, how can we use VR to experience healthy escapism?

SANCTUARY

Tradition has it that Jesus prayed every day, many times, while he was in Jerusalem, he took meditative sanctuary in the relative seclusion of the Garden of Gethsemane located on the Mount of Olives on the hillside across the valley from Jerusalem's western wall (this is part of our VR experience available under *Holy Land Tour*). Even Jesus needed some time off from his busy ministry. But in today's world, it is extremely difficult to find the time to walk, every day, to a secluded garden where we can meditate and pray. We have far more noise and clutter filling our daily lives than ever before and sometimes even the tools we use to escape the world have become the tools of marketing and advertising, adding even more noise and clutter.

All throughout history, people have used secluded sanctuaries for the purpose of getting away to relax and clear the mind. Churches, shrines, gardens, wildlife refuges and even hiking are all places people still use to clear their heads and find temporary relief. VR provides a quicker and more convenient way to travel without leaving your home (armchair travelers). Even tourism and real estate organizations now have sanctuary retreats in VR on their commercial websites. Of course, Bible VR focuses at the forefront on sanctuaries that are of biblical importance to the believer.

Stress is taking over our lives and it can be difficult to counter-command once it has taken over. It not only affects our work lives but our family lives as well. Constant pressure and fear about the future dominate our thoughts. This is when having a personal sanctuary can help take your mind off the stressors of life. Stress also causes health issues such as headaches, high blood pressure, ulcers and other more debilitating emotional and psychological maladies. They can manifest in your life in very nasty ways. So take the time off to relax. No, you don't have to go to a retreat that will cost you thousands of dollars and even more stress eating into your savings. You can use our devotionals and choose any of the locations you want to visit, and through VR, simply breath and meditate quietly. Even five minutes a day can help with your stress levels in the long run.

VR allows you to travel to places during a busy and hectic work and family life. Where home is supposed to be a place of peace, those who have families and children know that sometimes it can be anything but.

In our whirlwind lives, finding time to commit to going to places to relax is harder and harder. Which is why we created the *Devotionals* section in Bible VR. Singular VR experiences without tour guides or academics where you can be transported to a place and just be yourself.

When you are ready, taking it to the next level by incorporating meditation can really help, too.

MEDITATION

Bible VR does not claim to treat PTSD (Post Traumatic Stress Disorder) or other anxiety-related disorders. There are many companies using VR to develop treatments for those things. What Bible VR can be used for is meditation.

While meditation has its roots in Eastern religions, the Bible puts a high value on meditation (1 Timothy 4:15). However, it should be noted that instead of the Eastern way of repeating mantras or certain words and phrases, the Bible encourages meditation on the writings of the Bible. It invites us to meditate and focus on *"things that are true, righteous, pure, lovable, well-spoken-of, virtuous, and praiseworthy"* (Philippians 4:8).

This Book of Law shall not depart from your mouth, but you shall meditate on it day and night, so that you may be careful to do according to all that is written in it. For then you will make your way prosperous, and then you will have good success."

Joshua 1:8

You can utilize Bible VR and the many different locations we have available to sit down and meditate. It is your personal quiet time of reflection and understanding, all in places that have significant meanings to your devotional actions.

As mentioned before, you can use the *Devotional* sections in Bible VR, as they are quiet and free from any distractions. It's just you and your mind.

But do those VR meditations really work?

A recent study in VRET (VR Exposure Therapy) by Gonçalves, Raquel, Ana Lúcia Pedrozo, Evandro Silva Freire Coutinho, Ivan Figueira, and Paula Ventura has found that combining VR and actual exercise can give better psychological benefits than either method alone. VR is best used in conjunction with other healthy activities, which also includes spending time with family, friends and God. Again, *VR is a tool, not a means to an end.*

First-hand accounts from those who have tried VR meditation have yielded mixed results. Apart from immersive environments being an acquired taste, many purists believe that real meditation is an inward experience whereas meditating with VR is an outward one. This, however, goes against a study done in 2015 in an *Innovation in Medicine and Healthcare* conference paper that tested two groups of people, one of which utilized VR-based meditation. Their findings demonstrated that while both subjects reap positive benefits from meditation, VR-based subjects tested significantly better and experienced a more enhanced state of meditation than the other group.

However, we are not attempting to meditate using Eastern religion practices, we are going to meditate using what the Bible instructs us to do. The goal of meditation according to the Bible is to draw people closer to God. Instead of emptying the mind, in accordance with Eastern religions, Christian believers pour-in, filling the mind with God's truth. A much easier way to pour in truths is by meditating in places that are complementary to your particular meditation practices. Suppose you are meditating on a passage speaking on the birth of Jesus. You can use our VR experience '*Christmas in Bethlehem: Birthplace of Jesus*' to sit at the very spot when meditating, in order to focus your thoughts in the very place where the earliest tradition says he was born.

I will meditate on your precepts and fix my eyes on your ways."

Psalms 119:15

Fix your eyes on the Lord and tune out distractions, which is something that comes automatically when you are using a VR headset. Then simply focus on the VR experience for its duration (2-5 minutes). Meditate to focus on how God is speaking to you through his living and active Word. And don't forget to end with a prayer of thanks and supplication for clarity.

Different churches may preach, teach or encourage different ways of meditation. You may even find a meditating group, but ultimately, it is you who has to decide what works best for your meditative experience and what truly connects you with the Holy Spirit.

VR AS AN EDUCATIONAL TOOL

VR can be used as an educational tool both at home and at Church, and I will cover these in separate chapters. But what I want to cover, here, is the importance of using VR as an educational tool, both in how it impacts our learning and strengthens our beliefs.

In today's learning system, the primary tools of education are books and teachers. This applies to churches as well, where the primary book used is the Bible and the academic teacher is replaced by biblical teachers, your pastor or your priest. While we have many tools to help us better understand information, such as the internet, radio and audio/ visual materials, teaching methods today still rely on fact retention. This means you are presented with facts and it is your responsibility to retain them.

This can be particularly overwhelming to younger students, as they have to remember a lot of information in a short period of time. Remember, having an education is different from just being informed of facts and it is how you use that information and apply it that matters.

LEARNING THROUGH LIVING

It is often said that 'street smarts' are easier to learn and more important than 'book smarts.' Being 'street smart' is about hands-on experience rather than reading and memorizing words and factoids.

You can learn more about the Bible by living *in* it, rather than just reading it, despite the fact that reading and meditating on it is an important part of the devotional practice. No longer are you trying to tell somebody about the events that happened at Jacob's

Well, you can now take a field trip to the actual well where Jesus meets the Samarian woman. That's living it, rather than just reading about it.

What is equally important as just living it is the experience of being at the place where it all happened. This creates the grounding of your beliefs as you begin to live firsthand where these holy events have taken place. This is not merely a book of morals and tales, but actual history wrapped around the faith story. You know it because you were there living it, experiencing it and engaging in it. The feeling is remarkable!

ACTIVE RATHER THAN PASSIVE

Throughout history, students have sat in classrooms, staring at the teacher while he or she lectures the class. The same goes for clergy who preach during church services to an audience of silent listeners. This is a passive experience for learning where the student and/or churchgoer is sitting down simply absorbing information without participation or feedback.

In a high tech world where information comes at lightning speed and attention spans are getting shorter and shorter, the longer the learning times, the less a person will sit still to passively learn.

VR creates short but powerful ways to learn through an active experience. The audience can put on a headset and look around, actively participating in the locations and learning about history, archaeology, geography and cultural topics. By moving around within the VR experience, they begin to feel as though they are a part of the environment and just like taking a 'field trip', students are more excited because they are going to new places.

The difference between this and regular field trips, is that VR does not have the expense associated with it, nor the organizational nightmares, travel time, vehicular accommodations and other logistical issues.

With VR you can go anywhere in the safety of a classroom, church or the privacy of your home.

NO DISTRACTIONS

Classroom distractions are always a problem. People are constantly talking to each other, sharing things with each other, making noise or coming in and out of the classroom, amongst other things. VR provides a personal immersive environment without distractions, because the headset cuts off visual and audio aspects of reality, focusing the attention and concentration of the person using it.

The same benefits can apply without needing to worry about somebody running off, doing head counts, embarking and disembarking transportation vehicles and spending so much of the field trip time simply keeping up with the logistics.

Fewer distractions and more active experiences also mean more focus and learning about the historical sites and their Biblical importance. More focus leads to better retention as the person is experiencing it rather than just learning about it.

ALL LEARNING STYLES

There are many types of learning styles in this world. There is visual, aural, verbal and physical. Some people learn better in one style than others, so not everybody is the same. The current educational model experienced in schools and churches has been *verbal,* where words through speech and writing are the primary tools used for educating. Today, we incorporate some video and audio but they are mainly for supplementary uses rather than the main tools.

VR, as a tool, combines all learning styles into one. It is visual because you are looking around the locations. It is aural because you are hearing things and it's verbal as you use words to explain where you are. It is also physical because your brain tells your body you are there and experiencing it.

MULTIPLE USES

There are many uses for a single VR experience. Other than visiting important Biblical sites, people can also learn about different cultures and the role they play in Christianity. Sites such as *The Church of the Holy Sepulchre* showcase vast and different people of all cultures while *The Cenacle* (the place where The Last Supper was held) displays great history in architecture where teachers, pastors and priests can all discuss the history of the Bible, as well as the relevance and evolution of the changes in the architecture over the years.

The Church of St. Photina, where Jacob's Well is located, shows traditional Orthodox practices and how Pater Ioustinos' conducts his religious ceremonies.

VR's continued use in education points to a future where it will become a new cornerstone in how we learn and retain information.

In the 2017 Virtual Reality Brief, statistics of VR in education show that 97% of students would like to study a course in which VR is used. 97% of teachers say that students are excited to use VR, while 7 out of 10 teachers want to use experiences relevant to the material being covered. And while 80% of teachers have access to VR devices, only 6.87% of teachers actually have the ability to use it. It is my hope that the following sections on using VR in churches and homes will illuminate and inspire you with ideas on how to incorporate VR into your teaching experience.

USING VR IN CHURCH

The following section deals primarily with using VR in churches. While this is a helpful guide for pastors or priests who want to incorporate VR into their church, it can also be useful for the layperson who wants to introduce VR into their place of worship. For others, you may skip this section if you are more interested in using VR in your home with your children.

While many church leaders may still be hesitant about incorporating VR into their teaching and services for fear that the immersive factor might draw attention away from the church service, we are here to assure everyone that Bible VR was designed to complement a pastor's sermons rather than detract from them. As I have become repetitive in this little book, *Bible VR is a tool, not a means to an end.*

Several churches have worked with us to experiment the use of VR within their services, spanning the country from California and Arizona, to churches scattered throughout the Bible Belt in Florida, Texas and Indiana. We have found VR to be useful in many ways and we will help you with some ideas to get you started. Of course, we are always open to hear more stories about how Bible VR has been incorporated into your church, so do drop us a note and share some of your stories!

PRE-SERMONS

Pastors can use VR as a way to do some research especially before their sermons. Many times, you may be talking about specific events or places that appear in biblical passages and VR is a great way to 'travel' to those places to fully explore them before preaching a sermon. We know that the original Hebrew language can affect a Bible passage, using VR to show original locations will thus bring greater bearing within those same biblical passages and complement your sermons. This gives you a very clear idea not only about things on which you will be preaching, but experiencing these places is like going to Israel yourself and returning to share your experiences with your congregation.

Alternatively, some pastors have set up VR stations for under a few hundred dollars (most of the money goes into the smart phones to power up the content) and let their congregation see these locations that are going to be talked about in the day's sermon. This not only gives their congregation a head start, but encourages the congregation to come earlier, mingle and socialize together before the sermon begins. Biblically based churches are not just about preaching and teaching to a silent audience, they were meant to be places of fellowship for the congregation of like-minded believers, a place to gather that is separate from the rest of the world around them.

Utilizing VR creates something for them to talk about too. But more importantly, your congregation gets a chance to get a preview of your sermon, but it also lets them experience it for themselves first hand and talk with each other about their experiences. You will find that their grounding for your sermon will be much stronger as they have experienced it for themselves, too! Your words and their experience power and bond each other together.

Utilizing Bible VR has also been reported to help ease the integration of potential new members into the church, as it is a non-intrusive and fun way to introduce your sermons to them.

Another thing to consider doing, if you are setting up a VR booth in your church, is to purchase some disposable masks if the headsets are going to be shared amongst many people. These are disposable hygienic masks that people can wear over their eyes to protect against other people's sweat, skin oil, germs and other socially transferrable things. This mask is purely for sanitary purposes so that your congregation can enjoy VR without such concerns.

SERVICE

Bible VR is being utilized during service in a much different way. We do not expect the audience to be wearing headsets while you, the pastor, is preaching, as that would be incredibly distracting and potentially rude on our part to even suggest it. Ordained as a man of God, your words are a gift from him and we want Bible VR to complement your blessings, not take away from it.

Instead, use Bible VR with your current A/V (Audio / Visual) system to enhance your sermon experience. You can use Bible VR to show the locations that are relevant in your sermon through an additional device such as Apple TV or Google Chromecast, attaching it to your A/V system so that you can show to your congregation the places where the Biblical events of your sermon took place. Again, what this does is not only enhance your sermons, but it creates a stronger grounding to your teaching, lending it even more credibility. The impact of this is strongest with potential new members of the church who may be visiting for the first time, exploring how they can give their faith to Jesus. You are actually showing them all how the stories in the Bible are all real!

SUNDAY SCHOOL

Sunday schools are one of the most fun places to incorporate Bible VR. Younger children not only have the most fun using VR, but they are also learning something new as well.

Grounding their faith at an early age is not only a great way to start nurturing healthy beliefs, but also creates a fun and safe atmosphere for them to explore the foundations of their religion.

Mission VR is a collective group that has utilized Bible VR in sharing experiences with younger children. Quizzes and statistics show that even at a very young age, children are already retaining information. And when they can experience it, they grow with fewer doubts that the events in the Bible actually happened. Effectively, by allowing them to experience it themselves, we have turned their faith into belief.

One note of importance for Sunday school teachers is that, as with pastor sermons or personal home devotions, Bible VR is meant to complement your teachings. So, when children have experienced a part of the Holy Land associated with your teaching for that particular week, make sure that you spend time asking them questions, or finding fun things for them to do in VR that they can open up in discussions later on. You may ask them to do fun stuff such as looking for the candelabras that represent the three wisemen in the Church of Nativity in Bethlehem. VR is meant to be an experience we share and talk about, as one of our pillars of this entire endeavor is a belief in fostering not only personal devotions, but community and collective experiences.

Some parents may be concerned about children using VR because of their eyes. I will talk more about this in the following chapter, so please read it as it is very important. A lot of VR headsets warn against using it for children below 13. Much of that has to do with hardware design than actual safety for the eyes. These headsets do not have adjustable lens which means that it is impossible for the lens in the glasses to fit the smaller width of children's eyes, giving them an unsatisfactory VR experience. So please check your headsets before buying them.

The biggest worry about VR is obviously eye strain. Doctors generally enforce a strict rule of 10-minute breaks for every hour. However, Bible VR contents are only 2-5 minutes each. The real power in Bible VR is not to sit in it for hours at a time, but rather as a means to open up discussion amongst members of the church and family.

Always make sure that children are supervised at all times when using VR. Children are easily immersed faster than adults and may suddenly walk and run, not realizing that they are actually physically not in the location they are experiencing in the VR. In essence, they can easily become "blind" to their surroundings while wearing the VR headset. It is very easy to forget once you are in a VR experience that there is a real world beyond what you are seeing, especially for children.

A recommended headset for use with children is Google Cardboard. While the technology is the cheapest, literally made of cardboard, the strapless feature forces the child to hold the cardboard up with his hands, grounding a part of them in their actual physical surroundings.

And lastly, always sit down when using Bible VR. Because of the immersive factor in VR, standing up could cause some balance problems in kids – and even in some adults. While it is not in the least fatal, always make sure you take as many safety precautions as possible. The general rule of thumb is that there is no such thing as too much safety.

And if you are going to be sharing headsets – especially amongst the little germ factories we refer to as our children - as stated before, invest in some disposable hygiene masks. Their parents will thank you!

AFTER SERVICE

While people can still flock to experience your church's new VR booth, one of the greatest benefits you can give to your congregation is what happens *after* the service.

I have seen churches print out little devotionals that members of the congregation can take home. If they were to use Bible VR at home, having some spiritual guidance and devotionals or reflection cards from their pastors can not only help them with VR, but strengthen for them the pastor's sermon throughout the week.

This is a great way to carry on the relationship after Sunday. One of the greatest dilemmas faced by pastors, priests and church leaders is how soon the message presented on Sunday morning will fade from the minds of their congregation. A Christian's worship of God should not be limited to Sundays only, and Bible VR is an incredible tool to encourage them to get acquainted with The Holy Spirit throughout every day of the week. Use devotional cards and Bible VR to give them ideas on things to reflect upon for the week. In the descriptions of the VR videos, you can find some ideas, but come up with something unique on your own as you want your church to really feel your own uniqueness as a pastor. It's what makes you stand out!

An example of a Daily Devotional handed out at the end service for people to reflect on together for use with Bible VR.

You may contact your ambassador (if you have one) for Daily Devotionals from Bible VR that we can offer to you at no cost to help you get started. If you also want to be a Bible VR affiliated church, please register with us. Bible VR affiliated churches receive percentages of their member's subscriptions tithed back to your church. This is our way of making sure that the community and Kingdom of Christ supports each other!

PLEASE CONTACT US IF YOUR CHURCH IS USING VR SO WE MAY ADD YOU TO OUR LIST THAT WILL BE RELEASED IN THE NEXT BOOK EDITION AND ON OUR WEBSITE. THIS

You may contact us or any of our affiliates through our website http://www.bible-vr.com.

DEAILY DEVOTIONALS ARE ALSO AVAILABLE ON THE HARDBACK COPY OF THE BOOK

USING VR AT HOME WITH CHILDREN

Obviously, the biggest question on the minds of parents is, 'Is VR safe for my child?'. There are many questions surrounding this issue that I want to cover in detail here. While there are some who contend that VR is unsafe for children (especially for their underdeveloped eyes), Martin Banks, Professor of Optometry, Vision Science, Psychology and Neuroscience at the University of California, Berkeley has stated that he has seen no concrete evidence that a child of any certain age is adversely affected by wearing and using a VR headset.

Let's focus on a deeper understanding of what VR actually is so that we can best utilize it for our children without negatively affecting them in any way.

One of the chief concerns that parents have for their children would probably begin in the 1970s when one study by Susan Vitale, Ph.D, Mh.S found that near sightedness in those from ages 12 to 54 rose about 25% in the 70s and 41.6% in the late 1990s to early 2000s. There's a lot of evidence pointing to things such as reading and/or using the computer.

This damage occurs when a child focuses on something nearer to their eyes for lengthy periods of time. That concern is compounded when VR headsets seemingly focus on objects that are very close to the face. However, to understand the technology better, it is important to understand that VR actually works the opposite way. The focal lens in the VR headsets set the optics so that it makes the stimulus effectively far away from the face. Remember, your child is viewing worlds around him through the VR lens that sets his or her focus on objects and settings that are far away as opposed to reading something up close.

This is why we avoid putting text in our VR experiences or filming long VR sessions. We believe that VR experiences should be safe for all ages.

Other risks in virtual reality involve motion sickness. This is not only an issue for children but also for adults. This is when two different situations are happening at once. One is the time lag issue where an image appears to be jittery due to a slow computer processor, making people who are susceptible to motion sickness experience nausea or headaches. Another way motion sickness occurs is when you see motion in VR. Your mind is telling your body it is moving, but your body is saying 'I'M NOT!' This imbalance to the equilibrium causes motion sickness.

With Bible VR, we have practically eliminated these negative factors. We have filmed all our VR experiences on static cameras, which means as long as you are seated, you or your child will not experience any motion sickness. All of our experiences are shot in reality, so there is no need for the computer to process any 3D objects or simulated environments. Everything you see is real and requires only your internet connection for clarity.

So, let's get down to some fun you can have with Bible VR.

SPENDING TIME

One of our beliefs with Bible VR is that the technology should not isolate your child away from you, but rather bring your family closer together. While your child is immersed in Biblical worlds, the experience ends within a few minutes, but what the child gains from that is a sense of wonder and awe. Use that heightened emotion as a time to really teach your child more about the Bible. Start to educate them and discuss with them what they see.

As we have mentioned earlier in this book, what your child will experience is grounding. Your child has no problems believing that their house is real because they are experiencing it in their reality. They are grounded to it. When they experience Biblical lands through VR, they are also grounded to that. This is a time when you and your children can really connect. Ask them about what they just experienced. Ask them what they have just seen. Did they catch something you didn't? These are all engagements that are part of a bonding experience for you and your child.

Many children who grow up in Christian families become secular later in life. The trend of a decline in the Christian family is more prevalent in modern times. But this does not happen in Israel. In fact, the number of people believing in Abrahamic religions (Christianity, Judaism, Islam) has risen from 7.5M in 2009 to 8.1M in 2014 and 8.7M in 2017. Why is that? The reason is that children in Israel are grounded because in their 'backyard' lays the evidence of all the Holy Sites. It is their reality.

That's what Bible VR intends to bring to people who do not have the same access to the Holy Sites as people in Israel do. Grounding your children early protects them later from secular influence. Most children who grew up to be secular have no knowledge of what the Holy Land looks like. They are more easily susceptible to be swayed by other groundings such as science and atheism. This is much more possible because it is their reality and their experience, which creates their belief and grounds it.

Thus, it is very important to ground your child's faith early. This will create long-term benefits for not only your child, but your relationship with them. But again, take it in slow bits. Let them get excited about the next VR session. Let it be their choice. You will find that they will be much stronger Christians when they accept the Lord in their own heart, on their own, versus you imposing your beliefs on them.

PLAYING GAMES

Part of being a parent is also the level of creativity you can muster in creating fun things for your children to do. Bible VR has many VR experiences in the *Devotionals* section that are open and free spaces for exploration and fun. You can come up with games such as finding objects, looking for people or looking at architecture and nature. By linking with your child that the Bible is an exciting and fun experience, you are creating this healthy link between their perceptions and the Bible at a very early age.

Playing games is a great way to create bonding, as well, but not nearly as important as your child learning to see you as the authority. While we have movies for children to watch in VR and enjoy, we recommend that you spend time with your child on the other sections of Bible VR and govern their access as you would any other type of media usage.

THE AUTHORITY OF MEDIA

One of the most important but rarely talked about psychological effects on children today is the authority of media. You may not realize this, but the media has a much stronger authority than you because it provides outlets for your kids while profoundly working against you.

Consider that you allow your children to watch Disney movies. On the surface, they are very harmless and indeed entertaining. But look a little closer inside and you will see your child absorbing characteristics of the heroes being presented. Your children admire their heroes, mimicking their actions and role-playing them out. I talked about narrative transportation in the first chapter of this book and that is precisely what you are seeing when your child is doing when he idolizes and reenacts his heroes as seen in the movies, TV and other media

"But Disney's characters are fun and totally harmless." That is correct, but only to a certain degree. There are other subconscious issues about which we need to incorporate great care. Consider that most of Disney's characters are orphans or separated from their parents. From the classics such as Sleeping Beauty, Snow White, Bambi (his mother was shot by hunters in the movie!), The Lion King, and even Frozen, Disney characters constantly live their lives without need for the authority of their parental figures. Step-parents are almost always portrayed as evil and one even needs to pay close attention to how parents are portrayed in Disney movies as being, overall, ignorant to their children's needs and blind to their problems. While Disney characters can be fun and engaging on the surface, the relationship they have with their parents is not.

I'm not asking you to throw out all your Disney movies. What I am saying is that you need to balance what the children are watching and what they experience in reality.

You have to tell engaging stories and move your children emotionally. The Bible is a great place for that, and using Bible VR to enhance their experience level will create not only a stronger grounding to their beliefs, but establishes you as the authoritative figure in your child's emotional developing empathy. A child needs someone they can look up to as heroes and story-tellers. And they need to be drawing those things from their parents, and not from mainstream media.

This is why Bible VR was designed to be an open media for kids to enjoy. We do not put in our doctrines nor assault anybody with too much information. We don't want the Bible to be boring. We want it to be an experience that is filled with awe and shared together with the whole family. Bible VR was designed so that the most important aspect of media entertainment has to be contributed into its open-sourced media: that aspect is *you*.

In some ways, it is much tougher in the beginning for you than it is for a pastor. It is not because you do not have the pastor's knowledge of the Bible, it is because daily parenting can sometimes be a very intimidating thing, especially when it comes to providing healthy choices for your children's activities. Be aware: Your TV, tablets and computer games are waiting earnestly to take that responsibility away from you.

I believe that if you take things in small doses, slowly bring your child in closer to the Word, it will get easier. Pray to God for inspiration and wisdom to guide you in bringing up a child who will honor God and follow in their beliefs. God will answer your prayers because of your desire to do service to him.

SPREADING THE WORD

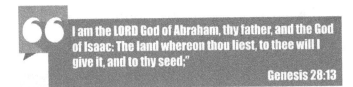

I am the LORD God of Abraham, thy father, and the God of Isaac: The land whereon thou liest, to thee will I give it, and to thy seed;"

Genesis 28:13

The underlying purpose of Bible VR is to spread the promise of God and share the life of Jesus with the world. Through Bible VR, Bible study, going to church and fellowshipping with your group, you can begin to live your life through the word of Jesus.

Being a Christian in a secular dominated world can be tough at times, so pray for the courage to stand in the gap and against the negative influences of the world. Spread the word of God despite what your inner voice (the Ego) tells you. Your ego will tell you "They'll think I'm weird" or "They won't hang around with me anymore" and all sorts of other excuses not to spread the Word or speak openly about your beliefs. But it is God's command to spread his Word. It is written in the Bible many times.

Persistence will be key. It is not easy to spread the good news because, well, nobody wants to believe such an easy thing such as 'God's love is free and attainable.' We are filled with so many instances of the media telling us we are not good enough, that we have to buy and consume products in order to feel better about ourselves. That is the reality for a lot of people and inside, they are suffering even though they wear the façade of a happy smile.

There are many ways you can use Bible VR to help people believe in the Word of God, or even enhance their faith. We have designed Bible VR to be a non-intrusive, fun way to get to know the Bible better and to experience the Promised Land. Notice that we never try to force anybody into believing anything, but rather, we show the beauty of the world and how traditions such as Christianity have contributed to it.

JUST FOR FUN

Because VR is still a very new and exciting technology, most people still have not yet given it a try. Wouldn't it be great if the first VR experience they had was faith based entertainment? That is something they are going to remember for the rest of their lives. As the saying goes "First impressions last."

You can use Bible VR without approaching any doctrines. Just use it to introduce some fun to show the biblical world to your friends. Soon, they will begin to ask questions like 'What is the Church of the Holy Sepulchre?' or 'Is Jesus' body REALLY in there?!'. They are going to be awestruck. Their beliefs are going to be shaken when they experience the truth and you will get a lot of questions. This is why I recommend for you to use Bible VR. But work with your pastor and church group for awhile before sharing it. There really is a lot in there to share.

The benefits of using fun to introduce the Bible using VR is that people are much more likely to be impressed with it than watching regular movies, audio or going to church. The secular world has already bombarded us with so much noise that what we need is something new and something fun to make the Word stand out. That's what Bible VR is all about.

Use fun events such as charities, picnics, movie nights and family get-togethers to really bring something new and exciting. Your creativity is unlimited. And Bible VR will always be available in your back pocket - or wherever you keep your phone.

And do not forget to do good and to share with others, for with such sacrifices God is pleased."
Hebrews 13:16

Be ready to spread the word by knowing the answers to three important questions and facts...

- What your life was like before you received Christ and became a Christian.

- How God has spoken to you and opened your eyes.

- What your life is like now.

Everybody has a testimony. Talk about your testimony in front of the mirror. Are you saying it with love and joy or are you crossing your arms and shrugging those lines?

When you speak about God, how you represent him is equally important. So make sure you go out there and share that love and joy with everybody else. Make them wonder what could possibly make this person (*you*) so happy all the time!

As you read this book and know that belief is the most potent force in the world, also understand that this applies to everybody. Secular or not, Atheism and Agnosticism are still considered to be systems of belief. Atheists believe that God does not exist and Agnostics can be completely bound by their seeking for answers. Do not try and force them out of their beliefs. It just won't work. It won't work on you, it won't work on them. Use tools at your disposal to share with them information and let them slowly cultivate that belief on their own. Whether you are using an evangecube, a spiritual presentation, Bible quotes or Bible VR, it's how you use the tools that matters most. You are sharing the Holy Spirit around. It is infinite in its abundance, and it is for everybody. Remember, people are drawn to people, not to people's beliefs.

AMBASSADORS

Bible VR launched a program in 2018 to include what we are calling, "Ambassadors." Many who take and use Bible VR to share with the world do so on their own time and at their own expense and we want to have a way to reward and help them.

We created the Ambassador program so that we can let people share in the profits from our company. Since profits have never been our priority, we want to give back to the community and help The Kingdom by contributing back to it.

Ambassadors receive a percentage of all subscribers they bring in. This means they are paid by the month depending on how many subscribers they sign up. Some ambassadors get paid monthly and by promoting its uses to churches, they receive enough every month to live on while they spread God's word without worrying about things like rent and bills.

If you would like to find out more about our program and how you can benefit from sharing The Word of God, please visit our website at http://www.bible-vr.com and we will gladly assist you.

LITTLE REMINDERS BIG GROUNDING

I've talked about grounding and what it can mean to your faith and beliefs. It is of utmost importance that we be grounded in our reality. Without grounding, we are people walking around in the haze of blind faith, easily shaken and disrupted.

If ye continue in the faith grounded and settled, and be not moved away from the hope of the gospel, which ye have heard, and which was preached to every creature which is under heaven; whereof I Paul am made a minister;"

Colossians 1:23

Our faith in the Gospel of Christ must be based upon a firm foundation. Without that, we are living life as foundering fledglings. Perseverance in our faith is the final affirmation to its authenticity. We must constantly be reminded of the Truth.

Truth is that stuff upon which you build your foundation and create your reality. What you tangibly see, hear, touch, and experience adds up to belief. This is what Bible VR is for. Habits and beliefs are synonymous with each other. Form great habits and your beliefs will follow suit in your every day life.

Here are the three main 'R's to forming your healthy journey with God.

REMINDERS

Use Bible VR to remind yourself of your experiences and what the Truth is. Use it to remind yourself where important events happened and meditate on them. Do it in little reminders so you do not overwhelm yourself and soon you will see that these little reminders add up to one solid grounded belief. You may use it once a day or even two or three times per week.

I do not recommend Bible VR to be used intensively and in large periods of time. As I have said many times, it is a tool for you to use; a tool to have in your pocket. Your Bible is the most important thing to have, but when you use it with various tools, it becomes more powerful and integrates itself into your life.

A phone, nowadays, is nearly useless without apps. All by itself, a phone is important, but the apps help maximize its efficiency and turn your phone from a communications device into a lifestyle device. A toolbox is nothing without a hammer or a screw driver. The most efficient toolboxes are those filled with many different tools in many different sizes. Your faith is similar. Ask yourself what tools do you have?

ROUTINE

Set aside some time to use Bible VR. Making it a part of your routine creates a framework of grounding your faith. Every successful person has a routine that they use. For many Christians, a simple routine such as praying before you eat creates deep ties of gratitude to God.

Routines are important for both children and adults because it helps us develop a sense of stability and order. It provides good structure and helps build good habits. It helps negate the need for willpower and motivation and builds momentum on your faith journey.

Make your routines small so you do not overwhelm yourself. Small routines add up to big things. Saving $10 a day adds up to thousands of dollars a year while running a mile a day adds up to 14 marathons a year. Set aside some time to use Bible VR. Doing it for even five minutes a day adds up to 30 hours a year spent with God's Promised Land, so much more than a typical tourist trip to the Holy Land.

REWARD

Give yourself a little reward each time you use Bible VR. They don't have to be big rewards. Thank God for opening your eyes to something new to fill your mind with wisdom and knowledge. You learn a little bit more about God's Kingdom and thank him for it.

Find a way to relax and pray to God with feelings of gratefulness. Meditate on things and cultivate a peaceful life. These are very small rewards, free to give yourself, but one needs only look around themselves to realize that peace in itself is a rare commodity in today's world.

These little rewards are no match, of course, for the big reward that's going to come. When you were going to buy a new car or house, did you not look through many articles, pamphlets and brochures about your soon-to-be new purchase and gloss all over it? What did it feel like when you finally took a seat in your new car or walked into your new house? Feels great, right? I don't remember anybody who buys a car or house without first looking at it in some form of a picture at the very least.

Bible VR is a lot like that. You are experiencing the Holy Land, the place where Jesus Christ will return in his prophesied second coming. You are experiencing where home will be. In some ways, you are looking at your future as Christians when Christ returns. You will know Jerusalem, you will know his home town, Nazareth. If you could ever talk to Jesus, think about all the things you already know about him. He can look upon you like an old friend who has visited and experienced his promised land.

Welcome home.

DEVOTIONALS

The following section and rest of the book is <u>unedited</u> and contributed by various authors, pastors and spiritual advisors. They are devotionals meant to help you in getting the most out of your VR experiences. With each devotional, you can reflect upon your VR experience and how to open up conversations both with yourself or your children.

It can also be used for Sunday Schools as ideas on what topics to discuss with children.

I thank you again for purchasing this book. May the Lord bless you with the wisdom and knowledge to understand his Word better.

Amen.

RUNNING AWAY FROM PROBLEMS

WATCH - Church of all Nations - The Garden of Gethsemane VR

All of us have have had problems in the course of our lives. Have you ever been stressed at work or at school? Have you or have you seen your parents worry about money? Some problems are bigger in our ever-changing and complex world, where we worry about life and death situations. In the middle of hard situations, the thought of running away always creep into my mind. *"Maybe this isn't meant for me, I should just quit now"*, *"This relationship is too much work, I would rather break it off now"* or even *"He/she is not my mother or father anymore"*. We get scared, we get frustrated and sometimes we procrastinate.

Jesus also faced hardship and agony, but he didn't run. Read <u>Luke 22:39-46</u> where Jesus *"being in agony he prayed more earnestly: and his sweat was as it were great drops of blood falling down to the ground"*. Jesus has no support from his disciples who were all asleep. And many of us sometimes feel in hardships, no one is there with us either.

So we run.

We run just like David ran from Saul, Moses fleeing Egypt or Jonah running away from the Lord. But what the Bible teaches us is that in the end, our only path to peace is through God. And the only way that path can be shown to you is through prayer - like what Jesus did.

He prayed and did not run. He bled instead of fled. For our sake, he chose to stay. He chose to suffer and die on the cross. But on Easter, God raised him up victorious.

Is there something you are running away from?

It could be an addiction. It could be from a relationship or stress at work. Whatever the case, watch Church of All Nations VR and explore where Jesus laid to pray in his most troubled time. Try to put yourself in his very shoes, at the very spot he laid.

Make no mistake hard times ARE hard, it will be painful for some. But by God's grace, he has a big plan for you. And like Jesus, when he was in The Garden of Gethsemane, through prayer he is revealed the answer to why he must do it. And through prayer, he eventually came out victorious. Today, make a list of all the things you can pray about today. Today, we do not turn our backs and run. Today, we stand up as Christians.

OTHER THOUGHTS

Do you know what kind of trees (some carbon dated to to be 2,300) dominate the Garden of Gethsemane?

The Church of All Nations is also known as the Basilica of Agony. Why do you think such a morbid name is given to it?

Do you think these trees are the only living witness to Jesus' final prayers before he was taken away?

WHY BAPTISM IS IMPORTANT

WATCH - Jesus Baptism Site - Qasr El Yahud

Have you been baptized as a Christian? Do you remember your baptism? Or the significance of this very important event in your journey as a Christian? I have been baptized twice. The first time was when I was a young child. The second time was as a young adult when I gave my heart to God.

"Go ye therefore, and teach all nations, baptizing them in the name of The Father, and of The Son, and of The Holy Ghost" teaches Matthew 28:19. The roots of Baptism lay many years before the founding of The Church with the Jews in ancient times.

For many Christians I spoke to, Baptism means the rebirth of their life as Christian. It is a symbol for the death of their sins and resurrection as a Christian. Majority of Christian do it publicly and at a young age of their lives. But it is more than that. Baptism is also an act of worship in the life of a Christian. It is not only obedience and submission, it is also a celebration.

Baptism is one of the rare form of ceremonies whose symbolism is about outward testimonies of their inward change in the Christian's life. As you are laid down into the water and pulled out, it symbolizes the death (going into water), burial (staying in the water) and resurrection (pulled out of the water).

Was your Baptism performed when you are an infant (for a lot of Christians)? Perhaps you are missing out on a true celebration, an important bookmark of your Christian life. If you are not baptized, even though you are

Christian, are you saying 'yes' to Jesus, but 'no' to baptism because it is too public?

What is Baptism to you? Do you have your own symbolism during your baptism ceremony? Baptism is just a ceremony until you give power to it through understanding what its power truly is. So today, I want you to give power to your Baptism… and mark it on your calendar to celebrate. We celebrate our birthday every year, why not our birthday as Christians!

OTHER THOUGHTS

Do you realize everyone is wearing white? It's an ancient tradition that those who are baptized in that robe, that when they die, they will be buried in that white robe. Why do you think so?

Why did John not want to Baptize Jesus at first? Would you do the same?

Why do you think the Baptism of Jesus is considered one of the most significant events in his life?

OBEDIENCE TO OUR LORD

WATCH - Basilica of Annunciation - House of Mary

Many Christians ask me 'How do I be obedient to God?', 'What does he want me to do?'. It is very hard to answer this question because your relationship with God is a very special one. How he talks to you differs for every person. 1 Peter 4:10-11 says *"As every man hath received the gift, even so minister the same one to another, as good stewards of the manifold grace of God. If any man speak, let him speak as the oracles of God; if any man minister, let him do it as the ability which God giveth: that God in all things may be glorified through Jesus Christ, to whom be praise and dominion for ever and ever. Amen"*

What this means is that God created us with special gifts, to serve him in obedience. And we are all different! When watching the Basilica of Annunciation, consider where you are. In front of you, through the gates is the site believed to be Mary's house, where the angel Gabriel appeared and announced to Mary that she is about to give birth to Jesus Christ (Luke 1:26-38). This was Mary's test of her obedience. Her first lesson in discipleship. And wow, what a responsibility!

But she will be rewarded for her obedience, as we all know! Her cousin, Elizabeth's husband, Zechariah, was punished when the angel Gabriel brings similar news of the birth of John the Baptist. But Mary was awarded and praised for her obedience.

So we come back to the question on how do you know what God has in store for you. Surely, not everybody is like Mary - a simple teenage girl suddenly thrust into a maternal role for the most important birth of our history. What makes Mary different? What did God choose Mary? And what will he choose for you?

The answer lies in The Bible. Inside the Bible is God's Word which he has shared to us how to become better servants of God. We all start small. Each small act of obedience is rewarded by something. Each small act of obedience follows with bigger responsibilities as Christians. We grow spiritually through small acts of obedience to his Word. And when you are ready, God will reveal to you the purpose he has in store for you.

Think about all the times you have acted in obedience. What about the those times you have not? Repentance, asking for forgiveness are just one of many ways you can reach out. We are all sinful beings. Through Jesus Christ we are saved. So what will you do today to show God your obedience?

OTHER THOUGHTS

The Roman Church believes the Annunciation with Gabriel took place in

Mary's House but the Greek Orthodox believes it's from a well. Why do you think they have two different beliefs?

What do you think Mary's actual house would have looked like?

Do you think Mary would have known or wanted such an impressive Basilica built in her name?

YOUR FAVORITE GIFT

WATCH - Birthplace of Jesus Christ - Church of Nativity

We all love to be given gifts. It makes us feel special, it makes us feel wanted. Think back about the last time somebody has given you a present. Think about how it felt like to open it. Seeing your present for the first time. It's the memories of getting the present as well that helps make a present much more valuable.

When watching this VR experience, we are reminded that we are standing in the exact spot of the greatest gift God has ever given to us: Jesus Christ. He is the gift that keeps on giving. The gift of Jesus is so pure that it does not discriminate. Many people buy presents and gifts for those they love or want to help, they would not buy gifts for their enemies or those who try to do harm to them. Yet God has given his gift to us even when we were his enemies. The Bible tells us, "But God commendeth his love towards us, in that, while we were yet sinners, Christ died for us" (Romans 5:8).

This present is like an unlimited box of chocolates that you can enjoy AND share it with everyone else (provided they like Chocolate). Life is beyond what is happening now and in the future. Life is about what happens beyond the grave. Life is about knowing God who made you and gave you the greatest gift you will ever receive.

So remember the day you receive Christ into your life. By remembering the value of this present given to us by God, we give it more power, more joy and more gratitude on the greatest gift ever given to us. But the most important question I will leave you with: how can you share this gift with others today?

OTHER THOUGHTS

Why is the spot that marks the birth of Jesus so low on the ground?

Why do you think the Church is owned by so many different faiths?

The Church is 1700 years old, why do you think it was built in the 4th Century and not right after Jesus died?

THE POWER OF OUR PASTORS

WATCH - Birthplace of John the Baptist - Ein Kerem

When I talk to a lot of Christians who claim they do not go to Church anymore, my big question on why brings up a common answer that people were jaded by their Pastors. Many feel that Christianity became more of a organization than a religious sanctuary and prefer to practice their faith on their own.

When looking at the Birthplace of John The Baptist in VR, we should take into account who John was, how important he is to Jesus' ministry. Now John's message in his time has also led a lot of people to believe he is the messiah. Even in John 3:28, he proclaims that he is not the Christ. John is merely a messenger of God, pointing to the real Christ. Does this sound familiar to you? A lot of us put importance in our Pastors that we feel let down when they do not meet our personal expectations on what they are supposed to be.

Jeremiah 3:15 says "*And I give you pastors according to mine heart, which shall feed you with knowledge and understanding*". Pastors are merely the conduits of God. They help point you in the right direction and nothing more.

Think about anytime you feel let down or disappointed by something your Pastor did. How can you correct your ways and your relationship with your Pastor? If he is a messenger that God has sent to you through him, what can you do more to pay attention to God's word in Church and less about what you can expect from the Pastor as a man?

OTHER THOUGHTS

What do you think people thought John was the Messiah?

If people thought John was the Messiah, how did both (Jesus and John as cousins) handle it amongst themselves?

Do you still think people today consider John to be a Messiah in other faiths

DOES SIZE MATTER

WATCH - Jesus feeds the masses - Church of Multiplication

My children love sports. From football to wrestling. One of the things they look after is their size and weight. They have to meet a certain weight class to play. Medals are awarded for who is bigger and better, or who is faster and more nimble. This brings up a question when I watch the VR video for Jesus feeds the masses in The Church of Multiplication (the spot that marks where the event occurred).

The whole story is very popular as it is one of 2 miracles (the other being his resurrection) that has appeared in all four gospels. But one thing that stuck out to me was in the gospels of John, it says that *"one of his disciples, Andrew, Simon Peter's brother, saith unto him, There is a lad here, which hath five barley loaves, and two small fishes"*

Lad?

One of the most important stories of Jesus' miracles started with a small boy! How amazing it is, that it all started with a small boy, and under the guiding hands of Jesus, fed 5000 people! And if you think feeding 5000 people doesn't interest you, I ask you to go back to the old testament where under God's guidance, David defeated Goliath as well! (<u>1 Samuel 17</u>)

What does this teach us? It teaches us that with God, all things are possible. It does not matter your size. So have you ever had a time when you felt small? Even if it has nothing to do with your size, have you felt people put you down? Think about those times, and pray today for God to lead you to the path of righteousness and victory! Because through him, all things are possible.

OTHER THOUGHTS

What other stories of the Bible can you remember that began with a little boy that rose up to greatness?

Do you know anybody facing the same defeat of feeling powerless? How can you encourage them today?

Why do you think the table over the block of limestone is called Table of The Lord?

BEING HUMILIATED

WATCH - Crucifixion of Jesus - Golgotha

At some point in your life, you would have felt humiliated. Whether it's by a co-worker, a family member or a friend. Humiliation hurts the heart and puts down the soul. It is a violation of human rights of dignity. Humiliation takes on several different forms, from body shaming, pointing out flaws in achievement, you name it. Someone has said or done something to hurt you at one point.

When looking at Golgotha VR, the holy site that marks the spot where Jesus was crucified, I cannot help but imagine the humiliation Jesus must have went through to save us from our sins. Crucifixion is so horrible I will not discuss the way people have died. He was humiliated when they make him bear the cross before they *"came unto a place called Golgotha, that is to say, a place of a skull, They gave him vinegar to*

*drink mingled with gall: and when he had tasted
thereof, he would not drink. And they crucified him,
and parted his garments, casting lots: that it might be
fulfilled which has spoken by the prophet, They parted
my garments among them, and upon my vesture did
they cast lots. And sitting down they watched him
there; and set up over his head his accusation written,*
"THIS IS JESUS, THE KING OF
JEWS" (Matthew 27:33-37).

What did Jesus do in his humiliation? Instead
of letting his spirit die, he pronounce
forgiveness for the soldiers, care for his
mother, amongst many others. Before he died,
he proclaimed in victory *"IT IS
FINISHED!"* (John 19:30). Through his
actions, we are saved. Forgiveness is now free.
Even after 2,000 years later, his crucifixion,
his humiliation still affects us too. Because
today we know we are saved. Today, think
about his humiliation and think about how it
has impacted you into the person you are
today. Think about who has humiliated you,
and like Jesus, how can you forgive them and

turn their actions into victory. With God, all things are possible!

OTHER THOUGHTS

For the sake of love, how much humiliation are you willing to bear? Compare that with Jesus' and the sacrifice he made for us.

When looking at the VR experience, look behind you - Why do you think so many Muslims come to pay their respects to Golgotha?

What do you think all the candles around Golgotha represent?

PASSION FOR OUR LORD

WATCH - John The Baptist's Church - Church of St. John

One of the hardest thing in life is finding your true calling. Your passion. Have you ever wondered that to do the Lord's work, you could be called upon to do something you hated to do? Whether it is your job, or going to school, we often find our lives surrounded by things we do not like to do. Could God call upon you to live the rest of your life (as per your calling) to do something you do not like to do?

Before we answer it, we should look at the life of John The Baptist. His ministry and work is now praised in the Church you see in the VR experience, John the Baptist Church. John was a preacher, who baptized people in his ministry. Unlike Abraham, Solomon or David, God never made him poor. As stated in <u>Mark</u>

1:4-6, *"John did baptize in the wilderness, and preach the baptism of repentance for the remission of sins. And there went out unto him all the land of Judaea, and they of Jerusalem, and were all baptized of him in the river of Jordan, confessing their sins. And John was clothed with camel's hair, and with a girdle of a skin about his loins; and he did eat locusts and wild honey;"*

As we can see, John did not even have nice things to wear. Could it be that he had to serve God as a poor man, living in harsh conditions and traveling the Holy Land? Indeed not, for you see, John has never once said (nor was there any account) of complaining about his state. HIs service to God is pure and with passion and love. When you are called upon to work for God, your true passion, love and service to him will muddle everything you deem to be misery. Through God's love, it will be the opposite.

Think about something in your life that you aren't happy about. Suppose you are doing something you think is God's work but you do not like it. Ask yourself whether God is really speaking to your heart, or are you doing it out of your own decisions. When God truly calls upon you to do your work, he will use your passions and talent to guide you. Everything else will be insignificant compared to what your journey with God will be. It's time to truly reflect!

OTHER THOUGHTS

Name something that you would love to do, how can you turn it around and use it for God's work?

Are you basing your current purpose in life based on material needs or wealth?

Write down what is stopping you today from pursuing your passions.

STAND AND GIVE

WATCH - The Last Supper Room - Cenacle

(Find this VR Experience in Devotionals Section)

Family holidays are one of my favorite times in the year. All over the world, families gather around to celebrate holidays with giant feasts. I know Thanksgiving is a day I stumble home full, stuffed and many leftover meals for the next week. Even in Jewish tradition, when they celebrate Yom Kippur (Day of Atonement) by fasting for the day, they have a pre-Yom Kippur feast as families and friends gather for a bountiful feast.

The idea behind preparing a feast is usually prepared by parents or the main caretakers of the family. Commonly, mothers would be the one preparing the huge feast for festive celebrations and we gather to eat her meal made with love and devotion.

When I stand in the middle of The Last Supper Room VR, this is the spot where Jesus and his disciples had their last meal before he was taken away. When you imagine what happened in here, images of Leonardo Da Vinci's famous painting come to mind. The image of Jesus in the middle, surrounded by disciples as he led the famous Last Supper.

But in the accounts of Matthew and John, we see an exact opposite. We see that Jesus himself organized the event (<u>Matthew 26:18-19</u>), he washed their feet (<u>John 13:4-17</u>), served them food and water (<u>Matthew 26:26-29</u>). He was depicted not as a savior, but as a servant. Truly, Jesus knew that power was not in sitting and receiving, but by standing and giving.

Those who stand and give, like my mother on a Thanksgiving meal, are those whom we look upon with adoration and love. Those who sit and receive, we usually meet them with scorn and judgment. That's why today everybody despises the government. This is why we despise celebrities who flaunt their wealth.

So what can you today to stand and give? Just one small act today, from a heart of love, can change your life. It does not have to be big like a dinner, but even a gesture of helping someone carry their school books, or to help a colleague with a deadline. The possibilities are endless.

OTHER THOUGHTS

What does it make you feel like when you give?

When you gift, do you give expecting something back, or give freely with love?

What do you think the significance of Jesus washing the feet of his disciples is?

DOES WORKING HARD PAY OFF

WATCH - Mary's Well - St. Gabriel's Church

I came across an article for many people who are protesting about minimum wage jobs. These are hard working people who feel that they are not getting paid enough to even survive on their own, let alone feed their families and loved ones. As economy grows, wages remain the same and many people are finding harder and harder to survive. The most common outcry is that the rich get richer and the poor get poorer.

While they certainly have a reason to be unhappy, wage increase is not the answer. Wage increase is just part of a solution. You see, when you put your value to a monetary number, your value WILL be a monetary number. There is a far more wealth and abundance around the universe and it is not men who provide it (even though they did invent money).

What does watching Mary's Well in Gabriel's church have to do with this? Consider this. Here is a young girl, barely in her teens doing hard labor work. Mary's well marks the spot where Mary would go down to draw water everyday to draw water. If you have ever carried a water bucket (not just for you, but your family), you know it can easily be very heavy. And of course, they did not have light plastic bottles to hold the water, we are talking heavy ceramic pots. Climbing up stairs, walking home… she did not have an easy life.

But we also know that any young girl who is accustomed to such heavy lifting in her time would also be fit and healthy for the long journey ahead of her. After all, she and Joseph would travel through hard terrain to Bethlehem while she is pregnant. See, God would not choose a girl who has all the luxuries in the world to be the mother of Jesus. God knew that Jesus would have a hard life and he needed a woman who not only works hard but is fit and healthy to nurture his son, Jesus Christ. If you were to hire movers to help move your house, would you ask the kids, the skinny frail looking men or choose the strong looking men to do it? You would choose the strong men, because they worked hard to gain the strength and now are qualified to move your heavy and precious valuables.

When you find yourself complaining about life and work, I want you to think about what muscle is God helping you build right now? The muscle could be physical, mental or even in the fast food employee flipping burgers, understanding how franchise operations work and maybe even use his skill to help the Church grow. What is your muscle? Build that muscle, because you could one day be called upon to do God's work.

OTHER THOUGHTS

If you don't know what your muscle is, think about where you feel your passions lie in?

How many ways have you felt in the past God has called you upon to do his work?

Compare your feelings after doing God's work versus everyday work. What's the difference?

MAKING A HABIT

WATCH - The Holy Land - Mount of Olives

We all have habits, I have mine when I get up to make a cup of coffee before I start my day. Some people go for a jog. Others simply have to run and get their favorite breakfast. Even during the day, we all have our habits. There are some bad habits people have. Spending money, watching pornography, smoking, the list goes on and on.

Even Jesus has habits, watching Mount of Olives VR, I am reminded in the scriptures that *"in the day time he was teaching in the template; and at night he went out, and abode in the mount that is called the mount of Olives"* (Luke 31:37). That's right, the very spot where you are looking around with your headset / phone is where Jesus would go to pray every night. Now that is a habit more people should pick up.

Of course, Mount of Olives is not a special place, no different from your room, even while you are at work. It happens to be the place where Jesus found to be quiet for his time with God. Any place can be a place of prayer, some places are more special than others.

Do you have a special place for your prayer? If you don't, where do you think could be a special place for you? Would you decorate it? How would you like it to look? Today may be a creative day of finding and creating that special place you talk to God. Have fun, be creative and make a habit to do something special everyday with your Creator!

OTHER THOUGHTS

What do you think Jesus prayed for every night and can you do the same thing?

Why do you think only Holy men are buried in the Mount of Olives?

What Christian symbol is most special to you and why?

CAN BAD THINGS TURN OUT GOOD?

WATCH - Church of all Nations - The Garden of Gethsemane VR

Have you ever wondered why bad things happened to us? Being fired from a job, a loved one passed away or even being back stabbed by a close friend or family member. Bad things happens to everybody, and our initial response is commonly to sink into sadness and victimhood. We blame others (or ourselves) for the bad things that happened. We sink into despair and depression. We don't know if we'll ever recover.

Crushing times are necessary times.

In The Garden of Gethsemane, Jesus was betrayed by Judas (John 18:1-2). He would be

taken away and later be crucified in Golgotha.
The age-old question that has kept millions
away from their connection with God creeps
into our mind *"Why does God all bad things to
happen to us?"*

As you watch your VR experience for The
Garden of Gethsemane, look around at the
Olive Trees. Think of the Olive fruit as a
spiritual fruit that accompanies the future.
The Olive is a bitter and hard fruit, but when
processed can turn into many things that
become useful such as Olive Oils that can be
used for many things such as cooking and
even has healing properties. Like the Olive
fruit, we must trust our Creator. For within its
tough and bitter exterior, he will help us see
the spiritual fruit that accompanies the future.

In his darkest times, Jesus did not fall into
victimhood. Instead, he prayed (Luke
22:39-46). He was in anguish such that his
sweat was like blood that came from his brow.

But God answered his prayers by giving him the wisdom to see into the future and know that in the end, he will rise up and be Victorious!

So is something troubling you today? Where can you find the hope and courage to go on. Inside Gethsemane is the reminder that prayer can help you through extremely difficult times. Victimhood is when you rest the problems upon your shoulders. Prayer is when you and God use your hardships as your spiritual journey together. Almost every story in the Bible (from Abraham to Moses, Joseph to David) begins with hardship. And it is only through Prayer and connection with our Creator can these hardships just be a guise under Miracles and Victory.

List down today all the bad things that has happened to you and the ways they eventually (or could eventually) work out. It is easier to see God's hands in problems that have come and gone. And let that list be a reminder to you the next time something bad happens... God has a plan for you!

OTHER THOUGHTS

Do you know what kind of trees (some carbon dated to to be 2,300) dominate the Garden of Gethsemane?

The Church of All Nations is also known as the Basilica of Agony. Why do you think such a morbid name is given to it?

Do you think these trees are the only living witness to Jesus' final prayers before he was taken away?

LEARNING FROM JESUS' BAPTISM

WATCH - Jesus Baptism Site - Qasr El Yahud

You know what being Baptized means. Other than a symbol of your obedience, it is also a symbol of repentance. When we visited (you can too by watching the video), a simple and humble site where Jesus was baptized, I overheard someone asking 'if Jesus was God, then why did he need to be baptized?'. I think the more proper question would be 'If Jesus was sinless, then why did he need to be baptized?'.

Read Matthew 3:11-15. It tells the story of why John the Baptist was taken aback and even considered unworthy of baptizing Jesus. And ponder upon the answer of Jesus (Matthew 3:15) for in there lies the answer!

Jesus was more than just publicly proclaiming the beginning of his ministries through his baptism in Qasr El Yahud. This is an event to be noted that has been prophesied by Isaiah, declaring people to repentance in preparation for their Messiah (Isaiah 40:3). When Jesus said *"fulfill all righteousness"* in his response to John, he is saying to the righteousness that he provides to all who come to him in exchange for their sins (repentance).

Another worthy thing to take from the important event of Jesus' Baptism is that without realizing it, John's reluctance to baptize Jesus also meant that he is fulfilling the role of a herald and the office of a prophet proclaiming the perfection of Jesus Christ, our Savior.

Jesus came into the world to identify with men, and to identify with men is to identify with sin. The baptism in Qasr El Yahud is very important for that is how he could purchase righteousness for us and eventually, free us from our sins. In the VR videos you will experience, you will see people bathing in white colored robes. Many come to Qasr El Yahud to wash their sins, pray for their sins. Many are baptized in those white colored robes and in some traditions, many use the same robes to be buried with them when they die.

The Baptism of Jesus sparked the first step to his redemptive plan for us. What else do you think he has done in this plan of his? How has it affected to you to this very day? Now that you have seen the waters where he was baptized in, you can imagine the incredible event that happened that still continues for you, through his Grace.

OTHER THOUGHTS

Do you realize everyone is wearing white? It's an ancient tradition that those who are baptized in that robe, that when they die, they will be buried in that white robe. Why do you think so?

Why did John not want to Baptize Jesus at first? Would you do the same?

Why do you think the Baptism of Jesus is considered one of the most significant events in his life?

WHEN OUR FAITH IS TESTED

WATCH - Basilica of Annunciation - House of Mary

Have you ever feel called to the Lord's work? Have you ever felt you had to do something but fear is holding you back? Often times, when God calls us to do his work, they are never easy tasks. Fear holds us back. Fear is the devil whispering into your ears 'Don't do it!'. You'll begin to think of all the things that could go wrong, friends you would lose .etc. Remember those feelings?

When the angel Gabriel visited Mary, she must have felt this way! Imagine if you were only a teenager and you were told that you would bear a child as a virgin. What would your parents say? We know in the Gospels that her fiancee (Joseph) almost left her, if Gabriel did not clarify it in his dreams. What would Mary be looked upon by those around her.

When watching the VR in the Basilica of Annunciation, think about how she must have felt, all alone in her decision. And remember, one of the first things Gabriel said to her was *"Fear not"*. Mary's faith is tested. But her faith in God is strong and unwavering. And her obedience may have led her to long hard journeys from Nazareth to Bethlehem and beyond. But we know her as the girl who changed the world!

When was the last time you felt your faith was tested? Usually we feel frightened when we meet something new and strange. We get confused and we know that things will never be the same again. Think about a situation in your life where you may have been avoiding change. Think about the change and pray about it. Are you being called to do God's work?

OTHER THOUGHTS

The Roman Church believes the Annunciation with Gabriel took place in Mary's House but the Greek Orthodox believes it's from a well. Why do you think they have two different beliefs?

What do you think Mary's actual house would have looked like?

Do you think Mary would have known or wanted such an impressive Basilica built in her name?

GIVING WHEN YOU ARE POOR

WATCH - Birthplace of Jesus Christ - Church of Nativity

One of the things that gets me down is when I do not have money to buy presents for my family and loved ones. I know what you are thinking, "it's not how much the gift costs, but the heart behind it". True, but what if I need to get a new computer for my children for their school and can't afford it. What if I can't afford new clothes? Giving and providing needs for my family is one of the staples of stability, security and love I can provide for my family.

Whenever I worry or stress about times like this, I remind myself I have already given them the most important gift in life. One that, when used correctly, is really all they ever need in life - 'Accepting Jesus Christ as their savior'.

For those who have found forgiveness of sins in Christ, there will one day be no more sickness, no more death, no more tears, no more division, no more tension.

So when looking at the VR experience, why is the room where Jesus was born so important? Because when we start to give the gift to others, this is where we start. The arrival of Jesus two-thousand years ago ensured that God had begun the process of reversing the curse of sin and recreating all things. It is the beginning of Jesus life, work, ministry, teachings and eventually his sacrifice.

Share the VR experience with your friends. Those who have not accepted Jesus. Show it to them and ask if they can guess what room they are watching. Look into their faces when you tell them the answer. Perhaps, when you see the look of being impressed in their eyes, this may begin your gift to your friend…

OTHER THOUGHTS

Why is the spot that marks the birth of Jesus so low on the ground?

Why do you think the Church is owned by so many different faiths?

The Church is 1700 years old, why do you think it was built in the 4th Century and not right after Jesus died?

POINTING TO OUR SAVIOUR

WATCH - Birthplace of John the Baptist - Ein Kerem

What are our tasks as Christians? One of the most important aspects of Christianity is to help spread 'The Good News'. As many have said 'poor beggars telling other beggars where they can find bread'. Not only should we point ourselves to God and Jesus Christ, we must also help others and point them to the way.

John The Baptist was born (as you can see in the VR experiences) and spent his life pointing to our savior. It was he who proclaim Jesus Christ the Messiah by baptizing him, even though many in his time considered him to be a Messiah. The shrine which marks his birth is important because we have to realize that John was born to be more than a baptist, but he was in fact the first prophet called upon by God, as predicted by Malachi 400 years ago. His birth was also foretold by another prophet. Isaiah 40:3-5 illustrates God had a plan by selecting John to be his special ambassador and will later send the angel Gabriel down to his father Zechariah to proclaim his birth.

We all know that John faithfully followed Jesus since he pointed to Jesus as our Messiah and Saviour. For that, Jesus has said (according to Matthew 11:11) *"Verily I say unto you, among them that are born of women there hath not risen a greater than John the Baptist"*

So ask yourself today how you can you be a better 'pointer' to our savior? What ideas can you come up with that exalts his name to the world and help spread 'The Good News'? Don't think you can be creative? Simply pray, and you'll be surprise how God can open up your creativity to spread his Message.

OTHER THOUGHTS

What do you think people thought John was the Messiah?

If people thought John was the Messiah, how did both (Jesus and John as cousins) handle it amongst themselves?

Do you still think people today consider John to be a Messiah in other faiths?

TURNING SMALL THINGS TO BIG

WATCH - Jesus feeds the masses - Church of Multiplication

Sometimes in life, everybody feels defeated. They do not have enough money, no friends (no popularity), they are so many things in life we may feel unworthy because we are not blessed with abundance. We see our friends live life with joy because they have bigger, better and nicer things. We wish we could have it too!

The feeding of the 5,000 is also known as the "miracles of five loaves and two fishes". It is one of the only miracles (the other being his resurrection) that was recorded in all four gospels (Matthew 14:13-21, Mark 6:31-44, Luke 9:10-17 and John 6:5-15). When watching the VR experience, seeing the rock where Jesus performed his miracle, I am reminded that God turns small things to big. When the masses were hungry and did not have enough to eat, God turn a small basket into a meal that fed a small town!

There is no such thing as a small thing for God. You could look at a drop of water, but God can turn that drop of water and part the sea for Moses! Through him, anything is possible. Through Jesus, God works his miracles and takes what seems insignificant and turns them into miracles. Sometimes, just because you have less, it could also mean God has the opportunity to bless you with more. If you had a thousand dollars and God gave you a hundred, it might seem like nothing. But if you had a dollar and God gave you a hundred, he has just multiplied your blessings a hundred times. This is why a lot of times people who are abundant are spoiled and ungrateful. They do not see blessings that God has given them.

Ask today in your prayers for the wisdom to see God's blessings to you. Write down a list throughout the day of all the little blessings God has given you. You will be surprised that at the end of the week, your little list suddenly looks like a big miracle!

OTHER THOUGHTS

What other stories of the Bible can you remember that began with a little boy that rose up to greatness?

Do you know anybody facing the same defeat of feeling powerless? How can you encourage them today?

Why do you think the table over the block of limestone is called Table of The Lord?

MOCKED FOR YOUR FAITH

WATCH - Crucifixion of Jesus - Golgotha

Every Christian has experienced it. Maybe it was a friend at school, or a co-worker, or even a family member, we were all mocked for our faith. Whether they practice another religion or they are atheist, we have all heard the familiar words such as "you know none of Christianity is true right?" or "you know that you are following blind faith?" are just one of the many things we have heard to test our faith.

When we watch Golgotha VR, we are instantly reminded of how Jesus died on the Cross. Today's devotional is to turn and look at the other 2 criminals who were hung on the other crosses beside Jesus. According to the accounts of Matthew and Mark, the two criminals mocked him. Here are people who are CRUCIFIED along with Jesus. They are DYING. Yet, they continued to mock him. Sounds familiar?

Like the two criminals, many people who aren't saved will continue to mock the faith of Christians all over the world until their dying breath. You might even begin to question your faith because you see their undying devotion to threaten you. You could argue back, you could fight back, or you could do what Jesus does. Ask for God to forgive them.

And then a miracle happened. After three hours, one of the thieves saw the truth for what it is. He had a change of heart and realized that Jesus was an amazing person. Through his actions, the thief began to realize that Jesus was truly the Messiah. And that's when he asked for forgiveness too. Jesus gave that to him and more! (Luke 23:43)

Who do you know in your life who has not been saved continue to mock you and your faith. Make a list of them and pray for their forgiveness today. If you see them, smile at them and silently utter a prayer for them. Because we can all learn from Jesus and even if they do not know it, they will soon come to realize that love conquers all.

OTHER THOUGHTS

For the sake of love, how much humiliation are you willing to bear? Compare that with Jesus' and the sacrifice he made for us.

When looking at the VR experience, look behind you - Why do you think so many Muslims come to pay their respects to Golgotha?

What do you think all the candles around Golgotha represent?

FIGHTING THE ENEMY

WATCH - John The Baptist's Church - Church of St. John

Enemies of Christ are everywhere. From those who mock the word of God, to indulging in immoral acts against God's will. Enemies come both if the face of people and also through our acts. As Christians, we face the enemy every day of our lives. The most cunning ones are those who use temptation to lead us astray. Others use threats to get what they want.

Much is know about the ministry of John the Baptist. Watching the VR experience of St. John's Church, one can easily see how exalted he was as a prophet and his life's work. But little is said about his death. Matthew 14:1-12 talks about John's death at the hands of Herod the thetrarch. Herod had John thrown into prison because he proclaimed against the incestuous relationship between him and Herodias and she plotted to have him thrown in prison, eventually beheaded.

His death is not uncommon even in today's world. Many Christians are still beheaded today at the hands of extremists groups such as isis. In fact, an article on Fox News, January 06, 2017 headlines that Christians are the most persecuted group in the world.

How do we fight the enemy and what can we learn from John The Baptist? John held steadfast in his conviction to God and his moral laws. His victory is joining God and Christ in heaven, his name is now exalted in his Church both in Christian / Jewish land as well as Muslim Mosques. Truly, he is one of the most exalted figures of Christianity and his name lives on to eternity.

Fear not when speaking for the word of God. To fear persecution is to fear everlasting life, which is the goal of our spirits. We sin when we keep our mouth shut because we are afraid. Fear is a sin cleverly disguised in excuses and lack of action. Think about how many lies you may have told in order to hide your faith to look good in front of others? Carefully ponder this throughout the day and pray for forgiveness each time you remember what you have done.

OTHER THOUGHTS

Name something that you would love to do, how can you turn it around and use it for God's work?

Are you basing your current purpose in life based on material needs or wealth?

Write down what is stopping you today from pursuing your passions.

FINDING MEANING IN THE BIBLE

WATCH - The Last Supper Room - Cenacle

Have you ever tried to find meaning in something? For example, think about the candles on your birthday cake? What do they mean? Blowing out the candles and making a wish is just one of many things we do that we find meaning in. Some people find meaning in shooting stars, lucky wishbones, dandelions. We find meaning in everything by mystifying what it represents.

So what do wishes have to do with The Last Supper Room. When I experience the place where Jesus and his disciples had the most famous meal in human history, I am reminded of Matthew's account of the event. Jesus said *"And as they were eating, Jesus took bread, and blessed it, and brake it, and gave it to the disciples,* and said, Take, eat: this is my body. And he took the cup, and gave thanks, and gave it to them, saying, Drink ye all of it: For this is my blood of the new testament, which is shed for many for the remission of sins" (Matthew 26:26-28).

Like our birthday candles (who were not made with the power to grant wishes), the bread and the cup (probably wine) are not made with any power. But they are a representation of something very holy. Today, we celebrate this symbolism in Communion. Today, we are reminded of what Jesus Christ did for us when he died on that cross.

Two people can break bread and drink wine. But one could be a meaningless ritual in Church, while another (fuel by his power and devotion to God), could truly celebrate with respect and reverence to God. Who do you think God blesses?

So today, think about anything that you could put more power into meaning. Think about something you have done so many times, it's like a tradition more than it is worship. How can you reconnect with God today?

OTHER THOUGHTS

What does it make you feel like when you give?

When you gift, do you give expecting something back, or give freely with love?

What do you think the significance of Jesus washing the feet of his disciples is?

SIMPLE THINGS WE TAKE FOR GRANTED

WATCH - Mary's Well - St. Gabriel's Church

I was sitting down at the table at a restaurant when I opened up a menu. As I started glancing through the menu, I do what probably everybody does: decide what I want to eat. Part of how I decide what to eat is the look down the menu and first decide what I don't want. The only time I looked up was when the waiter brought me a glass of water. And something came to me…

We do take the simple things in life for granted. We hardly ever think about drinking water. Water is available through turning on the faucet, as something provided free almost everywhere. When I look at Mary's Well VR, I am reminded that back in those days, things weren't so simple.

Mary was barely a teenager when she had to hike everyday with ceramic pots (Heavy!) just to draw well from the only town's water supply. Imagine how hard and laborious it must be JUST to get water. Today, we use water to brush our teeth, brew our coffee and we don't even think twice about it. Instead, we're more focused on whether our coffee is done the right way, whether our toothpaste is how we like it. We forget that water in itself is essential to life and we are blessed by how accessible we have it now.

There are many other simple things in life we take for granted. Look around you and think about the many ways that God has blessed us but yet we overlook it because we have it in abundance now compared to thousands of years ago. What other simple things have we taken for granted?

OTHER THOUGHTS

If you don't know what your muscle is, think about where you feel your passions lie in?

How many ways have you felt in the past God has called you upon to do his work?

Compare your feelings after doing God's work versus everyday work. What's the difference?

WHEN CHRIST RETURNS

WATCH - The Holy Land - Mount of Olives

We all know that Jesus Christ will return one day. This is news that even secular people know that we believe. Of course, the endless question is 'when'. Have you ever been asked that question in a mocking tone by someone else? Well, the Bible never says when, but I can tell you the Bible has said WHERE!

Watching the Mount of Olives VR, one would be struck by the fact that they are standing on a cemetery. Important Rabbis, Priests and Pastors have been buried in this land because it is significant to Jesus Christ returning. <u>Acts 1:12</u> states he will *"return unto Jerusalem from the mount called Olives, which is from Jerusalem a sabbath day's journey"*. This place is also significant for Jesus in that *"in the day time he was teaching in the template; and at night he went out, and abode in the mount that is called the mount of Olives"* (<u>Luke 31:37</u>).

But you won't have to be in Mount Olive when he returns. He will return with such loud thunderous triumph that all over the world we will hear it. But how amazing it is to know where it will all begin!

So the next time somebody asks you a question about Christ returning, you can answer them you know where he will be returning! The big question becomes "How will you be ready when he returns"? How are you going to take one more step to show your heart is fully committed to Jesus? Because you must be ready, you must look forward to it. To the day he stands again on the Mount of Olives!

OTHER THOUGHTS

What do you think Jesus prayed for every night and can you do the same thing?

Why do you think only Holy men are buried in the Mount of Olives?

What Christian symbol is most special to you and why?

DOES PRAYER REALLY HELP?

WATCH - Church of all Nations - The Garden of Gethsemane VR

Have you ever prayed hard and when you get no answers for your problems, you start to feel dejected? You wonder why do bad things happen to you, or why God allowed it to happen. Maybe you could even feel that he never answers your prayers.

In the Garden of Gethsemane, Jesus prayed (Luke 22:49-46) one last time before his crucifixion. If we were to take his prayers in the Garden at face value, God answered his prayers but having one of his disciples, Judas betray him (John 18:1-2) which ultimately led to his pain, suffering and death at the Cross.

When I speak to a lot of people, I realize that many people only pray when something bad has happened or is about to happen. In The Church of All Nations, it is also known as The Basilica of the Agony. You can observe in the VR experience the number of people who are also praying in there.

Many times, I hear about people complaining when bad things happens even after they have prayed hard. They wonder why God did not listen to them. But the truth is, it is not that God isn't listening to you, it is your pride that has got in the way of understanding and trusting his divine plan for you. We cannot know or even begin to understand his divine plan. All we have to do is pray for the wisdom and strength for these times.

I want you to think about the times you have prayed in anger. Think about how the stress muddles your ability to see through the problem. As you consider it, do you notice how many times anger, anxiety or stress never makes the problem any better? We forget that

we praying is not just a one way street.
Listening makes prayer become a connection.
When we pray, we have to connect with God.
To connect (like in any real life relationships),
it is more than just asking, it is listening and
doing as well.

So the next time you pray, quiet your mind
and see if you can listen to what God is trying
to say to you. He never speaks in loud
solutions, but in little whispers that come
together to turn into miracles. Think back
carefully when these moments have happened
to you. And when you observe The Garden
of Gethsemane, remember that Jesus prayed
there too, and in his hardest moments that
lead to his death, he became Victorious!

REMEMBERING YOUR BAPTISM

WATCH - Jesus Baptism Site - Qasr El Yahud

July 23rd is a very significant date for me. It is my birthday. July 23rd means something else to my colleague, the passing of his brother Phillip. July 23rd may mean something to you, or it may mean nothing to you. July 23rd is just a date. Until you give it some importance, that is all there is. When looking at Qar el Yahud, it may strike you that this simple location is where Jesus was baptized. This place may mean something significant to us, as Christian, but what about us? How important is our Baptism to us? What do we remember about our Baptism other than a public display of our new life as Christians?

In the end days, it is even foretold that
"Remember therefore from whence thou art fallen, and

repent, and do the first works' or else I would come unto thee quickly, and remove thy candlestick out of his place, except thou repent" (<u>Revelations 2:5</u>).

We celebrate our birthdays so quickly, we celebrate things like Thanksgiving and pay our respects to many other holidays with celebrations, food, drinks .etc. But yet, many of us do not celebrate an important hallmark to our faith (and new life), which is the day of our Baptism. When you stepped into salvation, you cross from death to life. You must consider yourself dead to sin and alive to God in Christ Jesus (<u>Romans 6:10-11</u>). Jesus' death separated your sins from you. Now THAT'S worth celebrating!

What if we were to celebrate our Baptism day every year? Perhaps you and your friends can get together to throw together a small get together and help each other remember your baptisms. Do you remember who was there for your baptism? Do you remember the prayers, the hugs, the warm welcome into God's kingdom? Baptisms mark very good and happy memories for a lot of Christians. What can you do today to honor that wonderful memory?

OTHER THOUGHTS

Do you realize everyone is wearing white? It's an ancient tradition that those who are baptized in that robe, that when they die, they will be buried in that white robe. Why do you think so?

Why did John not want to Baptize Jesus at first? Would you do the same?

Why do you think the Baptism of Jesus is considered one of the most significant events in his life?

BLESSINGS WITHOUT SUFFERING

WATCH - Basilica of Annunciation - House of Mary

Is it possible to be blessed without some form of suffering? All the books in the Bible of heroes, Messiahs and Prophets all depict forms of suffering before ascension and victory. Blessings seem to come after suffering. But why does it have to be this way?

Consider Mary, who was visited by the angel Gabriel in her house (you can see where it is in the Basilica of Annunciation VR). His task to her would surely shame and tarnish her reputation both for herself and family. She would take long hard journeys to Bethlehem. And if being born in the manger was not enough, they had to flee the following day to save Jesus' life.

Watch the VR and see her Basilica where she lived. She would not have had financial prosperity, comfort or recognition in her village. Think about how she must have felt during then. But yet, she is most favored and blessed amongst women in the eyes of God.

Hardship is inevitable. Think about times in your life now where you face hardships. Could you be in financial hardships? Is home a place where you experience much arguments and distress? Why are you going through it?

One of the lessons we can learn from Mary is that despite hardships, if we can draw from God's strengths and his provisions. If we can do what God wants (ask in Prayer) instead of what we think we want in life, then we too will be favored and blessed amongst man. That's what we can learn from Mary.

Remember, God never said it will be easy. But he said he will always be with us!

Today, pray and reflect on your hard times and ask God for the wisdom, strength to see you through. Write down any small thoughts or emotions that come to you during the day. You will find that the Holy Spirit has always been there with you!

OTHER THOUGHTS

The Roman Church believes the Annunciation with Gabriel took place in Mary's House but the Greek Orthodox believes it's from a well. Why do you think they have two different beliefs?

What do you think Mary's actual house would have looked like?

Do you think Mary would have known or wanted such an impressive Basilica built in her name?

THE POWER OF HUMILITY

WATCH - Birthplace of Jesus Christ - Church of Nativity

When people brag, when they talk about how amazing they are (even if they are true), can put off others around him. Nobody likes one who brags, or is cocky. Being humble is seen not only as a strength, but impresses those around you. It makes people want to be around you.

When watching the VR experience, I am always reminded what it means to be humble. Jesus, our savior, deserves to be born with big celebration and the world thrown at his feet. But think about how he was born - In a manger. Think about how the place would have smelled. There is another VR experience in our movies section where you can see a re-enactment of that scene. The place is dark, lonely, no Santa Claus, no presents, no Christmas Trees. But yet, his birth will continue to be celebrated every year for over 2 thousand years.

Jesus' life after his birth held the very same principles. He does not brag about his ministries or miracles he perform. Indeed, he did not even brag about how simple and humble his miracle birth from a virgin has been.

So reflect back when we were bragging or trying to show off. Think about how we can catch ourselves in the future and learn to be humble like Jesus. Is there something you can do instead to turn your achievements into something that could be useful to people around you? What can you do today to be more humble in the future?

OTHER THOUGHTS

Why is the spot that marks the birth of Jesus so low on the ground?

Why do you think the Church is owned by so many different faiths?

The Church is 1700 years old, why do you think it was built in the 4th Century and not right after Jesus died?

STRENGTH IN OUR FAMILY

WATCH - Birthplace of John the Baptist - Ein Kerem

Where did the words 'Sibling Rivalry' come from? Have you ever felt competitive with members of your family? Whether it is a simple game of tag football or maybe competitive with school grades or even how much one person makes in salary versus another? We've all been competitive, sometimes a little jealous when somebody is perceived to be better than us.

Looking at the VR experience and seeing where John was born, I am reminded that he was born as a close family to Jesus Christ (Luke 1:36). Now it must be mentioned that John himself is regarded as a prophet and some even considered him a Messiah. Matthew 3:5-6 mentions *"Then went out to him*

Jerusalem, and all Judeaea, and all the region round about Jordan, and were baptized of him in Jordan, confessing their sins. So did John try to 'one-up' Jesus and be competitive? Nope, instead he did the opposite and proclaim Jesus to be the true Messiah. John was born to Zechariah and Elizabeth who is the cousin of Mary (mother of Jesus). Even if Jesus may not directly be his sibling, John was very steadfast in proclamation of Jesus as The Christ.

What would John gain by pointing to Jesus Christ as our savior and even following him through his ministries across tough terrains and weather? Think about how his humility has saved all of us. But what about you?

John proved that the strength in one can be accentuated by the bond in family and through the word of God. What can you do today to help your other family members be stronger with God? How can you work with your family (instead of being competitive) to help spread the Message? Even if you may not get along with some of your family members, what you do today with them could change the lives of others around them.

OTHER THOUGHTS

What do you think people thought John was the Messiah?

If people thought John was the Messiah, how did both (Jesus and John as cousins) handle it amongst themselves?

Do you still think people today consider John to be a Messiah in other faiths?

WHAT YOU GIVE, YOU RECEIVE

WATCH - Jesus feeds the masses - Church of Multiplication

Some people call it Karma. I don't like to use that word because it is usually associated with some form of 'punishment'. A lot of people have asked me about giving and receiving. Many people today don't tithe to the Church. They could be financially strained, or they see no value in giving money when what they need to do is save in our dire times. People also don't give emotionally as well. They protect themselves in the heart in case anybody hurts them. But what can we learn about giving and receiving?

I'm reminded when I see the spot where Jesus feed 5,000 people with just 5 loaves and 2 fishes. Watching the VR experiences that marks the exact spot, remind yourself that

Jesus took leftovers and turn it into a meal for a large village. And not only did Jesus feed the masses, there was still leftover fish and loaves!

Through Jesus, God multiplied. Because Jesus gave himself to God, he was able to perform these miracles. What can you give to God today for him to multiply? Do you have talent in something that he can multiply? Do you have money that he can multiply (tithe to your Church is a great way to do it!). Whatever you give to God, he will multiply. From friendships, money, relationships and family. There is nothing he cannot multiply for you!

But before I end this devotional, let me just remind that when you give to God, give it with gratefulness, humbleness and with your heart. Do not give if your heart is sour. Do not tithe to the Church if you were to walk out after services and feel distressed about giving away all your money (that's why tithing is only a small percentage of your money).

Before you give anything to God, ask yourself what your attitude is? Are you doing it only so you can get more, or are you sincerely giving it away to God because everything in your life is also his.

OTHER THOUGHTS

What other stories of the Bible can you remember that began with a little boy that rose up to greatness?

Do you know anybody facing the same defeat of feeling powerless? How can you encourage them today?

Why do you think the table over the block of limestone is called Table of The Lord?

PAYING BACK YOUR DEBTS

WATCH - Crucifixion of Jesus - Golgotha

Debts can be more about money. Children can sometimes owe their parents chores, or doing their homework. But most of us surely know what debt is. We are happy when payday comes because we can pay back any money we owe on credit cards, or mortgages. But is there a debt spiritually we are not aware of?

Sins are our debts. We commit sins when we do follow the moral laws of God. We are all sinners every day of our lives. So how do we pay back our spiritual debts? The good news is that paying back spiritual debts is a lot easier than we think.

Watching Golgotha VR, we can all be reminded that Jesus died on that very same spot so that our sins would be forgiven. He has suffered and died on the cross so that our sinful lives and debt can be repaid. He paid it for us! Who else do you know would do that? A rich relative or friend might help you out of a debt, but that's only because they could afford it. Jesus gave his life for us! Jesus moved us from the old testament ways of animal and children sacrifices to pay back the debt of sin into an act of love and compassion. Through his death, the world is changed!

I want you to think today about the sins you have made. What can you do to turn it around? Asking for forgiveness is just step one. What can you do to turn your sins into acts of righteousness?

OTHER THOUGHTS

For the sake of love, how much humiliation are you willing to bear? Compare that with Jesus' and the sacrifice he made for us.

When looking at the VR experience, look behind you - Why do you think so many Muslims come to pay their respects to Golgotha?

What do you think all the candles around Golgotha represent?

HOW DO WE DEFINE OURSELVES

WATCH - John The Baptist's Church - Church of St. John

When I ask people to describe themselves, they usually begin by saying 'My name is ABC, I am an (accountant) (teacher) (student at XYZ school). In today's society, we often define ourselves by the job, profession or family relations. But is it who we really are?

Looking at The Church of St. John, I am reminded that John's ministry is one that is described as "a voice in the wilderness". Matthew 3:3 states *"For this is he that was spoken of by the prophet Esaias, saying, The Voice of one crying in the wilderness, Prepare ye the way of the Lord, make his paths straight"*. What this means is that John is merely an instrument to the word of God.

Christ is the word of God. But like John, we can start defining ourselves not in the job, profession or family relations that we do, but as instruments for the word of God. Truly, there is nothing more powerful. No job nor vocation can beat that!

How do you define yourself? And how can we start to change this mindset? Ask in your prayers today how can you be an instrument to God's word? How can you be like John and allow God to use you in his divine plan for you.

OTHER THOUGHTS

Name something that you would love to do, how can you turn it around and use it for God's work?

Are you basing your current purpose in life based on material needs or wealth?

Write down what is stopping you today from pursuing your passions.

DEFENSE MECHANISM

WATCH - The Last Supper Room - Cenacle

Have you ever panic and realized you have not studied for an exam and pour into your books the night before? Remember that feeling when you know your boss is about to fire someone so you work extra hard in order to make sure that person isn't you? When times are tough, have you tried to look for another job? These are all defense mechanism, things we do during hard times to protect ourselves.

Take a look at the VR experience for The Last Supper Room. This is the room where Jesus held the famous last meal before he was taken away to be crucified. Imagine the feeling as Jesus said *"Verily I say unto you, that one of you shall betray me"* (<u>Matthew 26:21</u>) Jesus knew this would be his last meal. His disciples know it will be their last meal with him. Now in today's world (even in prisons), Jesus would have been given everything he wanted. The biggest feast or the biggest praise. His disciples would be doing everything they can to make his night happy.

Instead...

Jesus washed the feet of his disciples himself. It would be a simple meal of bread and a cup that he served to his disciples himself. Surely, this is the action of a servant! Not a Savior! Jesus knew what will happen, but instead of having a defense mechanism, he simply served. This isn't about Judas (the famous betrayer), but also about Peter when Jesus predicted that *"before the cock shall not crow, till thou hast denied me thrice"*, meaning that before sunlight, Peter would deny Jesus as his savior. His own disciple!

Jesus did it because he knew that he would later rise up victorious. Jesus did it because he knew his Father in Heaven had a plan for him. This is what it means to be Christian. To understand that whatever happens, God has a plan for you.

When was the last time you panicked about something? You were afraid of something? Losing a job, failing an exam, or losing your house? Pray today. Ask God for the strength to see his divine plan for you. With him, all things are possible!

OTHER THOUGHTS

What does it make you feel like when you give?

When you gift, do you give expecting something back, or give freely with love?

What do you think the significance of Jesus washing the feet of his disciples is?

SIMPLE PEOPLE ARE MEANT FOR GREAT THINGS

WATCH - Mary's Well - St. Gabriel's Church

Why are we so attracted to celebrities? Is it because of some 'talent' or a character 'trait' they have that makes them heroes. Why do we enjoy reading things about these people? Is it because they inspire us? Is it because they do things or have things we wish we have?

We hardly look at the person walking down the street in plain simple clothes, but we stop to look at magazines or the TV playing at a restaurant. We enjoy watching sports and seeing athletes accomplish great feats of almost superhuman abilities.

When I see the VR experience for Mary's Well, I'm wondering if I would notice the young girl who came every day to this very well, the only well in town, to draw water for her family. This simple girl, would later become the most important woman in history. But she was just a simple girl from a small home who came here everyday to get simple necessities like water.

The Bible never says Mary is anyone but an ordinary girl. But it is her righteousness and obedience that allowed God to use her in an extraordinary way. The Angel Gabriel said that *"Thou that art highly favored, the Lord is with thee: blessed art thou among women"* (<u>Luke 1:28</u>). So while we are all enamored by celebrities and athletes, we sometimes forget that deep down within us, we all have that power in the eyes of God. He sees them as no special than you or me.

So how are you preparing your life when God calls upon you to do his work? Do you believe he could be calling you to do something extraordinary? If you don't, I want you to think about Mary. Even she did not prepare herself in anyway for such a responsibility of bearing Jesus. But she was righteous and obedient. That's something you can have this very minute. So what's your next move?

OTHER THOUGHTS

If you don't know what your muscle is, think about where you feel your passions lie in?

How many ways have you felt in the past God has called you upon to do his work?

Compare your feelings after doing God's work versus everyday work. What's the difference?

PREPARING TO GO HOME

WATCH - The Holy Land - Mount of Olives

Going to the Israel to shoot with the Bible VR team was both eye opening and inspiring. We are all in love with the country, despite it being dangerous several times. After a month of hiking and shooting VR experiences, we are all ready to go home. We are ready to sleep in our own beds, eat a hot meal with our family and take a long shower at home. But as we were shooting in Mount of Olives, I can't help but ask the question "Which home?"

The Mount of Olives is regarded as the place where Jesus will return. Acts 1:12 states he will *"return unto Jerusalem from the mount called Olives, which is from Jerusalem a sabbath day's journey"*. He will return and he will take us home together with him, up there with our creator! My heart leap for joy. This is the true second coming. This is truly going home.

Our homes may be destroyed by fire, taken by the government or robbed by a criminal. But our REAL home up there in Heaven can never be taken away from us, or destroyed by another. This is what it is truly like to KNOW you have a home - FOREVER! If that doesn't make you excited to go home, I don't know what else will.

So while we are packing our bags to go home from Israel, I ask myself this and want to share this question with you. How are we preparing today to go back to Heaven with Jesus? What kind of 'packing' do we have to do? How can we surrender ourselves to Jesus to prepare for this glorious day? The answers alone can fill a book! But I want you to dedicate today in thinking about this, praying about it and acting on it! Because you never know if tomorrow is the day!

ABOUT THE AUTHOR

Dr. Pearry Teo is the founder and lead designer of Bible VR. Dr. Teo started his career as an authority in VR creating experiences for movie studios before turning his duties as a Christian back to God by starting Bible VR. Independently funded, he travelled across Egypt, Jordan and Israel to bring back VR experiences while finishing his doctorate in psychology, ministry and education. He continues to travel across the world in search for the living truth. Dr. Teo currently lives in Los Angeles where he is an ordained minister and certified counselor.